Contents

Justice in My Tears	1
Persona non grata	5
Farisani Airways	11
The vote against reason	13
Born Criminal	15
Free all round, captive all round	17
My country South Africa	18
Government gone crazy	19
Defy Satan, defy tyranny	21
Permanent Tourists	23
You tried to isolate me: November 21-22, 1986	25
Thank God Tshenu is back	27
Apartheid faith	29
Who is my neighbor?	30
On the Jericho Road	31
Here we stand!	33
Kid's questions are the toughest	35
Informer	37
Stooge	38
Trees	39
Crying is for men	41
If I were a god	42
I love my country so much	43
Botha you are not alone	44
In hell all are equal	45
The Lord is my shepherd Psalm 23 in Pietermaritzburg and Howick March 13-June 4, 1977	46
The Lord is my shepherd Psalm 23 Second Incarceration October 21, 1977, to January 21, 1978	46
The Lord is my shepherd Psalm 23 from the bottom of hell November 18, 1981, to June 1, 1982	47
The Lord is my shepherd Psalm 23 from the land of manna and quail November 21, 1986-January 30, 1987	47
This place is dirty	49
Farewell to innocence	57
I am not a politician	58
Were it the other way round	59

Sankambe the Sly	60
There is nothing for nothing: Dialogue between a pig and a hen	61
Sermon on Table Mountain	62
On that day	66
Gonna reap what you sow	67
What's ability without opportunity?	68
Same—Same—Same everywhere!	70
Hit harder	71
Ike	72
Zion songs in foreign lands	74
Confessor of Christ Award: Reply	77
What's life without fear?	79
Alone in company	80
Rest in peace	82
In our own right	83
Klein Kaatjies* and Little Kittens	84
Existence in transit	85
Do black laborers feel?	87
At theological college	88
Natural pairs	89
My congregant My Judas Iscariot	90
Prisoner outside Prison walls	91
The Beast man	93
We owe these women	95
Think small—talk small—act small	97
Amnesty International	99
Killer permits	101
Moving into the net	103
Little big ones	104
Mother love	105
Man beast	107
It is not a choice between east and west	109
Tit for tat and butter for fat	110
Are you an honorary God O Lord?	111
Too clean	112
Thank God I am free	113
Can't be so bad	114
Sin once and for all in one spurt of rage	116
I feel like giving in	117
Living for my children I must die for them	118
What am I fighting for?	119
Keep your medicines	120
At a road block	121

Moon	122
The Sun	123
Rain	124
Greed	125
Created in the image of evil desire	126
Legal Circus	127
Singing Chains: A visit to detained Pastor Molefe Tsele	129
My sword	131
Change me now	132
Not in your image	133
Sands that break and stick	134
Now I am ready to die	135
Freedom of speech	136
From A to D	137
Have you ever	138
Now's your turn	139
We are beaten if those we uphold lose	140
If we	141
Not meant for each other	143
A multiracial tree	145
Home	146
Culture of evil, culture of loss	147
Only one way to freedom	149
Public enemy number one	150
Hostages: Mother Roxelelwa: We've lost	153
Dear God: a telephone call to heaven	154
Victory is certain	157
Enough for everybody	158
Does it matter	159
Above the law	160
The mind of a detainee	161
From the mouth of those that sow in our midst	163
On my heels	166
Bloodstains in my hand	167
Home-sick	168

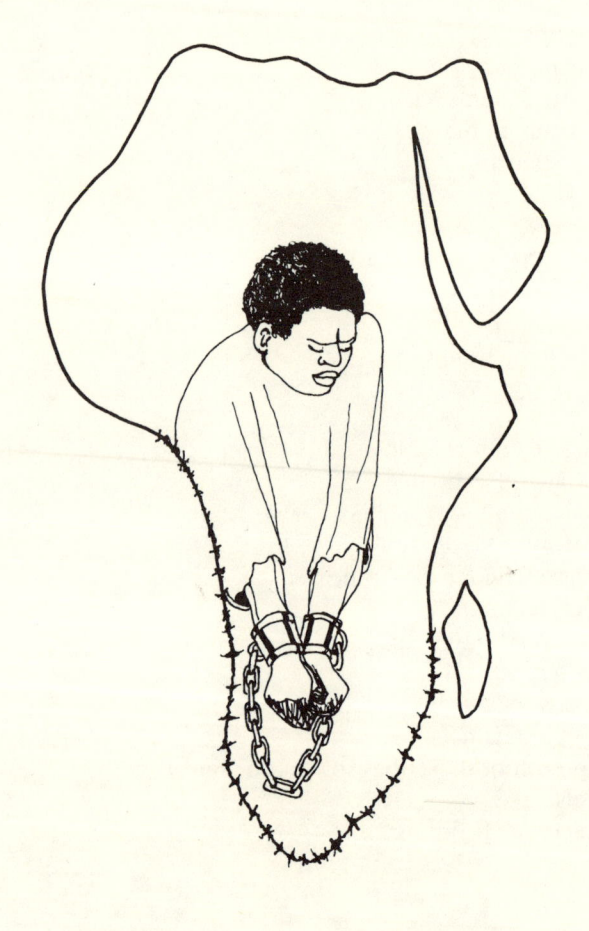

W Knezovich

Justice in My Tears

Message to the reader: In South Africa we are not allowed to think; we are not allowed to see; we are not allowed to hear; we are not allowed to feel; we are not allowed to smell; we are not allowed to taste.

The white racist government knows that nature cannot obey their laws. They therefore tolerate us if we

> think but do not express our thoughts;
> see but do not perceive;
> hear but do not try to understand;
> feel pain but do not cry;
> smell apartheid but do not vomit;
> taste freedom abroad but do not aspire to be free;
> know we are human but believe we have tails;
> accept homeland citizenship but know we are South Africans;
> worship God but serve Mammon and Satan.

Mamatho spoke against Van Jaarsveld's prescribed history book and got three percent in the midyear exam.

We wrote poems in "Focus on the L.T.C."* and earned the wrath of white pie-in-the-sky theologians.

Our ideas appeared in the book "Detente" and were honored by a banning order.

We spoke up our minds in our magazine "Flashlight" the first issue was banned; the second was banned; subsequent issues were banned.

Before then, organizations and black leaders were banned.

In September 1977 nineteen democratic organizations and newspapers travelled the same road.

---

*Lutheran Theological College.

In the cemetary of ideas, in Pretoria's censorship coffins, shouts the epitaph: HERE LIES, SILENCED FOR THE MOMENT, THE BEST OF THE IDEAS AND DREAMS OF SOUTH AFRICA'S SONS AND DAUGHTERS, DENIED ACCESS TO THE NATION THEY WOULD SAVE!!

What do children of detained parents, Pretoria-made orphans, think and say and do?

What goes on in the mind of a detainee, or of a dispossessed people?

What are the fears and the hopes, the joys and the sorrows, the frustrations and aspirations of a trampled people?

Is there any symbolic gesture from nature that may nourish the mind, nurse the wounds and nurture the hope?

Does God, whose other name is the ANSWER, have answers for the apartheid questions that have bedeviled his province South Africa for years?

I have spoken.
I have preached.
I have lectured.
I have written prose.
   AS
Many of my countrymen and women have done.
   BUT
None of these avenues have been able to fathom the mind of a beleagured man; a beleagured family; a beleagured nation; an existence in-transit between despair and hope, defeat and victory, hate and love, persecution and admiration, composure and anger, frustration and determination, LIFE and DEATH—the battle to be!

This book is dedicated to those who appreciate an appetizer before their meal, who do not forget the hungry as they eat, and who when they drink their washdown juice, do not forget to cry for those who are thirsty:
   Some are called "Africans". Perhaps Negroids?
   Some are called "Coloreds." Perhaps mixed blood?
   Some are called "Indians." Perhaps Mongoloids?
   Some are called "Whites." Perhaps Caucasoids?
                             IF
I were not a law-abiding citizen, I would name them:
MANDELA
BOESAK
NAIDO
NAUDE
The people, the workers, the church: ALL AFRICANS—ALL AFRIKANERS—ALL SOUTH AFRICANS.

August 16, 1987
New York, NY

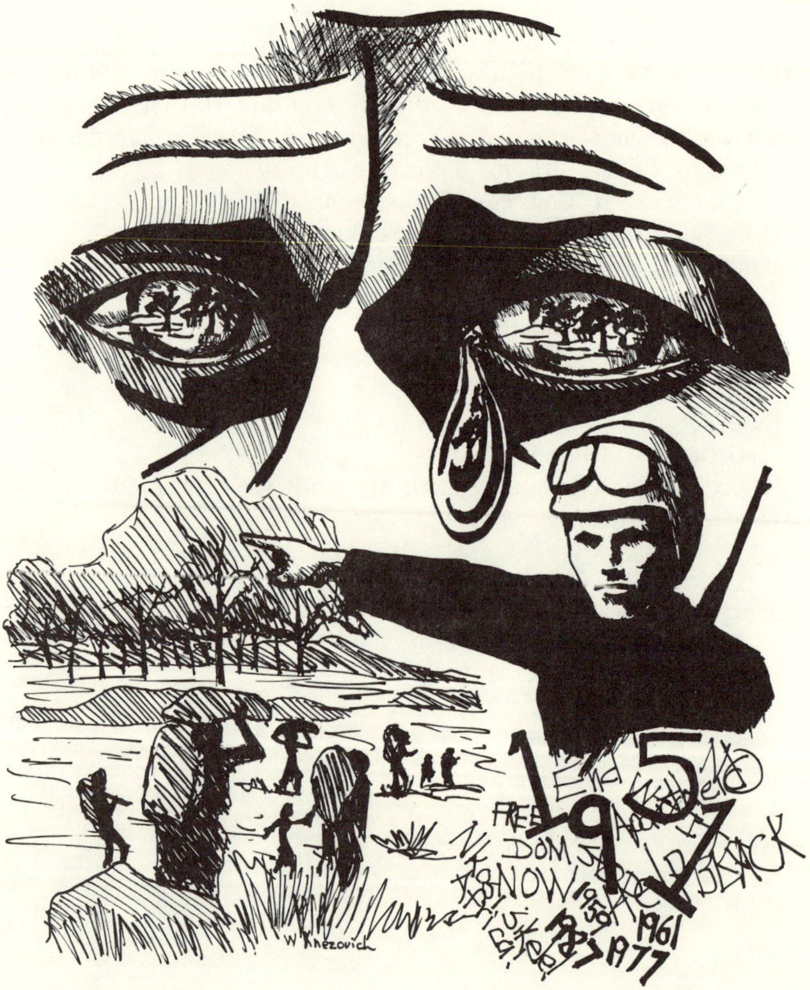
FREE
DOM
NOW
BLACK
1961
1977
W Knezovich

Persona non grata

Swongozwi my fertile land,
Swongozwi our great mountain!
    The plains of Tshapinda, a fertile carpet at our feet:
    The fields are life to our people,
    The wild fruits health to our young!
Cursed 1951:
      By government decree,
      Authority without reason,
      Legislation without feeling,
      All blacks must move!
Will the powerful compensate the powerless?
    Take your houses if you can,
    Take your fields, soil, and water!
The voice of power is the voice of truth,
The voice of government that of God!
    Bye Swongozwi my fertile land,
    In white hands till freedom day,
    Vox populi vox deo!
Epitaph:
      We shall miss our fields,
      Our orchards we shall see no more.
      We shall miss our waters,
      Our fruits we shall pick no more.
      We shall miss our fauna and flora,
      Our honey we shall eat no more.
      We shall miss our history,
      We shall miss our past.
      We shall miss our roots,
      We shall miss our graves.
      We shall miss our dead,
      We shall miss our baboons,
      We shall miss our monkeys.
In white hands till freedom day,
Nkosi sikelel Africa!
Thabeni our gracious land,

Shall you comfort us to forget Swongozwi our fertile land?
    Valleys and hills not so green,
    Fields and rivers not so full of life,
    What future have you in store for our young?
Cursed 1959:
    By government decree,
    Authority without reason,
    Legislation without feeling,
    All blacks must move!
Will the rich compensate the poor?
    Take your souls if you can;
    Take not your cattle, chickens, and goats!
The voice of proclamation is the voice of good,
The voice of Pretoria is the voice of heaven!
    Rest in peace Thabeni land of losses,
    In white greed till the day of sharing,
    The voice of sufferers is the voice of winners!
Epitaph:
    We shall miss your cattle,
    Our goats and chickens we shall see no more.
    We shall miss your valleys and hills,
    Our rivers we shall swim no more.
    We shall miss your neighbours Tshifhawe and Tshilata,
    Our traditional beer we shall drink no more.
    We have lost our right to farm,
    We have lost our right to eat.
    We have lost access to water,
    We have lost our right to drink.
    Our dead shall miss the living,
    Our living shall miss the dead.
    Your birds shall miss our crops,
    No bird meat for our young anymore.
In totalitarian hands till Uhuru day,
In the cry of the victim lives the seed of victory!
Mbabada our new home of sand and stone,
How do you compare with Tshapinda the land of plenty?
    Flat land and thorn brushes everywhere,
    Watermelons and kaffircorn not so good for me.
    What's buried beneath these grey futureless sands?
Cursed 1961:
    By government decree,
    Authority without reason,
    Legislation without feeling,

All blacks must be piled on top of one another!
Will the settled compensate the unsettled?
   Carry your hunger and thirst to the Promised Land,
   The land of starvation and unmarked graves!
The voice of continuous removals is the voice of order,
The label of impermanence our permanent status!
   See you no more Mbabada cruel land,
   May sandstorms sweep your valleys few and barren,
   The voice in the desert is the dessert of hope!
Epitaph:
   We shall miss our neighbours' milk,
   Our melons and millet we shall relish no more.
   We shall miss your thorns and sand dunes,
   Our kids shall miss your polluted waters.
   Venomous adder, poisonous scorpion, will you do without us?
   We are tired of the beer of oppression,
   We are tired of farming the rocks.
   We are tired of hunger and thirst,
   We are tired of burying our kith and kin.
   We are tired of belonging nowhere:
   Today citizens of here,
   Tomorrow citizens of over there,
   Next year citizens of in-between.
   Scare-crows, non-entities we are!
In perpetual motion till Mandela Day,
The voice of Pollsmoor, blueprint for the future!
Madodonga land of hope and despair,
Mbabada your distant cousin or twin sister?
   Exposed to winds of wrath and drought of death,
   Open to whirlwinds for years beyond the pale.
   Any life beneath your sands and hope above the ground?
Cursed 1977:
   By government decree,
   By power without limit,
   Legislation without mandate,
   Consolidate Venda into one block!
Will the boer empathize with the bantu?
   Forsake your ideas and utopian dreams,
   Enjoy your freedom in the Venda of plenty!
The mind of Pretoria knows what's good for you,
Amandla! Power! 1979 freedom year to serve the master!
   Shall we now leave our tamed desert?
   Without wind and whirlwind shall we survive?

The voice of defiance is our train to freedom,
Enough is enough, prison or freedom;
    We are here to stay; we are here to pray;
    We are here to pray, here to act!
    The voice of terror is not the voice of the shepherd!
Epitaph:
        We miss our fields;
        We miss our orchards;
        We miss our rivers;
        We miss our fruits;
        We miss our gardens;
        We miss our cattle;
        We miss our past;
        We miss our freedom, our being.
        Where is our humanity Pretoria?
In suspension till Dagon's fall,
Minority power, usurper's power, majority voice that of government!
South Africa my country black and beautiful,
South Africa home for all black and white.
Citizenship for all who love and adore you,
Franchise for all men and women mature and colourless.
My one undivided democratic non-racial South Africa!
Cursed 1987: January 28:
    I have to inform you
    that your exemption from the visa
    requirements as laid down
    in section 40(1) of the admission
    of Persons to the Republic Regulation Act,
    1972 (Act 59 of 1972) which you enjoy
    as a Venda citizen has been
    withdrawn.
    This means that before you can
    again enter the Republic of South Africa
    you will have to be in possession of
    a visa . . . .
    Should you in the future arrive at a
    South African port of entry without
    a visa
    You will not be permitted to enter.
    Furthermore your exemption from
    the requirements to be in possession
    of a temporary residence permit
    in terms of section 2(b) of

the Aliens Act of 1937 (Act 1 of 1937)
has also been withdrawn
Yours faithfully
E. Barber
Pp Director-general
/AEW
Department of Home Affairs: PRETORIA

Oh Lord, my God!
Can a guest become a host?
How does an alien alienate the native?
May a European deafricanise me?

Jesus, oh my saviour!
What's Van Riebeeck up to?
Who is P.W. of all the Bothas?
In whose country is the home affairs department?

Oh Lord, my God,
Hold my tears lest they fall on foreign soil:
   My guest has turned my history upside down.
   My story he has twisted inside out!

A true brother to the good Samaritan:
I found Botha stranded in the Hague and gave him land.
I found Le Grange wounded and nursed him.
Was it a trap my Lord?

Heunis was naked and I dressed him.
Viljoen was illiterate and I taught him.
Magnus Malan was afraid and I taught him courage.
Now I must reap the bullets my Lord?

E. Barber was hungry and I fed him/her.
Verwoerd was a nazi and I prayed for him.
Vorster made empty promises and I believed him.
Is every government from you my Lord?

Treurnicht and Marais were strangers and I housed them.
A few blacks hated whites and I taught them love.
They pushed me out; I pulled them in,
What are you doing to me O God?

Christ, my Lord, must we give the other cheek?
Must we go back to the homelands?
Why should they not go back to Europe?
Must we love them while they hate us?

We must be peaceful you say my Lord,
While they practice violence every day?
Must we respect their lives, oh God,
While they desecrate our funerals every day?

Must we accept exile like you my Lord,
Stay in Egypt till the angel's call?
Why not fight our way home,
Or will you take us back today?

We pray for their repentance;
They pray for guns and cannon;
We pray for humanity's freedom;
They pray for white survival.

What's your time O God?
Past midnight, my God?
Thirty minutes past liberation hour?
Four hundred years past salvation hour?

Shall we take matters into our hands?
Shall we map out our own destiny?
Shall we solve this problem the human way?
Or is there still room for your way?

Oh Lord, Omniscience:
I know I do not know.
I know that I know.
Shall my knowledge alone free me?
I need you to back my know-how.
Of one thing I'm certain: I need you now.

Farisani Airways

Seventy days behind bars,
Sixty-nine nights dark and dull.
The nights of fear are over,
Restrictions the new order.

Six days of hard work by church and lawyer,
Five nights full of sorrow and despair.
Every cloud has a silver lining,
Transit visa available for you.

Away, six hundred kilometers far far away,
To Britain from Jan Smuts airport.
Six, five, four and half hours madness drive
Shall I make it, my Lord?

"Are you Bishop Farisani, sir,
Lutheran by faith and black by belief?
Four p.m. come back for your visa,
I need time every time I work."

I shall not wait for the hour of despair;
Tonight I shall not miss my flight of hope.
My flesh is not your steak,
Truly my health is at stake.

"You come back eleven o'clock, my bishop,
By then your visa will be here for you."
Why call prophets terrorists?
Why call me bishop which I'm not?

"Before you go too far Bishop Farisani,
Here's a form formed for you."
Defrocked of my inalienable citizenship,
Let the form be filled with ink of tears.

"Are you back so soon my bishop?
Get me two photos identical,
Get them quick and fast
No photos, no move on our part!"

Slow down Dean Farisani,
We have wives young and beautiful,
Two sons and three daughters, five mouths to feed,
Two widows and five orphans at a go?

"Are you back so soon my bishop?
We shall need an hour or two."
Always enough time to do evil,
Always no time to do good.

Ten. Eleven. Twelve. Five past twelve!
"There's your visa and your Krish Naidoo.
In five minutes already at Beuster,
8 kilometers behind us."

No seat in United Air,
No room in Letaba airways,
No space in Venda air,
Angels have wings; today I shall have mine.

Check in the luggage Regina,
Passengers Makongoza and Sihlangu fasten your seat belts.
Welcome aboard Farisani airways,
Behind the instrument panel is Captain Jesus.

Stop! Stop! St---o---p! SSttoppp!
Guilty! Guilty! Guilty of speeding!
Subverting the road, subverting the nation.
Twenty-five minutes writing a twenty-rand ticket my Lord?

Six hundred kilometers away,
Four and half hours at our disposal.
100 • 120 • 140 • 160 • 180 kilometers per hour
Nearer my God to thee, nearer to thee?

Watch not the speedometer friends,
Look not at the flying trees.
Watch the petrol gauge,
Christ is behind the wheel.

Tshakhuma. Levubu. Louis Trichardt. Botlokwa
Pietersburg. Treurnichtland. Pretoria
Shall we make it friends?
    Almost.

Jan Smuts airport. Customs. Into the bird.
   Shall we thank the opel for the speed?
   Whose skills were behind the wheel?
   They delayed me; he delayed British Airways
Fly fast. Fly Farisani Airways
Fly safe. Fly Christ's airways!

The vote against reason

Botha's win is Botha's loss;
Treurnicht's gain is profit in vanity.
123 seats against reason is a long suicide note,
  22 rightwing seats an insult against reason.
  2 daring independents down the drain,
    1 to suffocate in parliament gas chambers.
  19 Progs without support of kith and kin,
    Shall Waterberg call the tune?

1909 they all voted against reason;
1910 they united against reason;
1913 they voted against the land;
1936 they voted against the landless;
1948 they voted against humanity;
1961 they voted against democracy;
1982 they voted against time;
    Shall Rajbansi call the tune?

Whose poll was this my countrymen?
Against whom this poll, women of South Africa?
  A poll against Africa,
  A poll against blackness,
  A poll against life,
  A poll against habeas corpus,
  A poll against freedom.
    Shall the winners win the day?

Eighty-two percent voted against reason;
Rightwingers had a field day;
On the far right they had an open season;
Ultrarightists appeared in the will.
  A poll for detention without trial,
  A poll for the state of emergency,
  A poll for death.
    Shall Connie Mulder call the tune?

Adult whites have the right to vote,
White idiots shape the government.
Adult Blacks have no rights.
The ballot box is surely not for them:
  We shall vote with our feet;
  We shall vote with our hands;

Bombs and strike action?
   Is the ballot reserved for whites?

Colin Eglin and the Progs are no more,
Power for fools, coffins for the wise!
Why oppose Botha for doing wrong?
C.P. Shall oppose him for not wronging enough!
   Coffins for democracy everywhere,
   Political funerals for ten liberals a day,
   One blow to reason, ten blows to hope.
      Shall doom call the tune?

One million one hundred thousand apartheid mandate,
Six hundred thousand votes Botha's apartheid not good enough,
Three hundred thousand Progs fall from grace.
Twenty-five million black votes disqualified:
   In the democratic land of South Africa,
   In civilized Western society,
   Christian and Capitalist God's own land,
      Shall Satan call the tune?

Botha has won; Botha has power:
Doom has come; doom has death.
The lie is king; truth must serve.
Terror shall reign; decency must fade.

We have no vote, but a future;
Our future is bright.
Mandela Prisoner King, Botha King Prisoner,
Twenty-five million shall call the tune,
   God shall tune the future.
      Amen.

Born Criminal

Born black, I'm born criminal,
Born Zulu, I'm born with hoodoo.
Born in homeland, I'm born wrong.
Born of mixed blood, mixed fortunes await me.
   Born of wrong color,
   Born of wrong mother,
   Born of wrong father,
   Born of wrong tribe,
Created by a wrong god for wrong reasons!

My residence in Hillbrow, I'm an illegal resident,
To be in Pretoria is a violation of the Group Areas Act,
South Africa, my home, is not for aliens.
I float in the air, guilty of air pollutions act.
   Foxes have holes.
   Birds of the air have nests.
   Dogs have colors, but don't have to care.
   We have to carry our color every day.
Created baboons in human disguise!

Married, but I have no permit to live with my wife.
Solemnized with no right to consumate,
Husband and wife on a marriage certificate,
Found guilty of sharing the same bed.
   White men are male,
   White women are female,
   What God has put together,
   No man should put asunder.

Talented with skill, but use of skill denied;
Given mind and intellect, but others think for me;
Willing to learn and know, yet kept in darkness and ignorance;
Potential to reach the sky, but bound to earth by apartheid norm.
   Pilot material, black must jump from the tree;
   Train engineer, ride on a millipede;
   Steward in South African Airways, domestic service by force;
Created to be what I should not be!

We shall live by our sweat.
Idlers have no right to food.
Thus says the Old Testament,
Thus says the New Testament.

We are guilty of working day and night,
Guilty of doing white work,
Guilty of laboring in wrong areas,
Guilty of aspiring to white wages.
Created from same clay, but not to suffer and lust!

Conceive, multiply, and fill the land;
Subdue and control it;
Rule over the fish, animals wild and domestic;
Be human all the way!
    Punished for being too many;
    Penalized for embracing spouses black and beautiful,
    Sentenced for overcrowding thirteen percent of South Africa;
    Fined for blackening black Africa;
Created to suffer for the Creator's paint!

We have minds and moods that inhabit our being;
Dreams and visions criss-cross our aspirations;
We plead guilty to being human;
Innocence would shame our God.
    We shall defend our guilty being;
    We shall reside in the wrong places;
    We shall kiss our spouses against the law;
    We shall fight for our right to be black;
Created free, we shall work to make our world free!

Free all round, captive all round

Power-hungry, power-drunk, unfree!
  Alone in power,
  Alone in greed,
  Alone in fear,
  Alone in the laager,
  Alone in despair,
  White South Africa!

Hungry for freedom, thirsty for justice, free!
  Alone in the cell,
  Alone behind the walls,
  Together in hope,
  Together in the battle,
  Together in the struggle,
  Black South Africa!

Captives of tradition, enslaved to ideology, handcuffed!
  Western, strangers among Westerners,
  Democrats, not at home with democracy,
  Subscribers to rule of law, violaters of habeas corpus,
  Proponents of dialogue, experts at monologue,
  Haters of neighbor, lovers of self,
  Racist South Africa!

Born of tradition, independent of tradition, free!
  Denied humanity, yet most human,
  Robbed of education, yet well informed,
  Stripped of togetherness, yet united,
  Hated and hounded, yet loving and hugging,
  Outgunned and gunned down, yet coming and winning,
  Indomitable, Uhuru-hungry, black South Africa!

Worshippers of law and order, slaves of the law!
  Morning cereal offering to the god of gunpowder,
  Noon peace offering to the god of prejudice,
  Burnt sacrifice to the god of Verwoerd, Vorster and Botha,
  Human sacrifice to the god of cross-border aggression,
  Passover feast to the god of Blood river,
  Anti-black, white South Africa!

My country South Africa

South Africa is my country:
Her sun is my sun!
Her rain is my rain!
Her drought is my drought!
This is my South Africa . . . Mine!

South Africa, my land of birth:
Look at her forests—they are mine!
Look at every single tree—they are my trees!
Look at her dead grass—that's also mine!
Forever my South Africa . . . Mine.

South Africa, the land of my life:
I swim in your rivers!
I hunt in your bushes!
I play in your dust!
Oh my home South Africa . . . Mine.

South Africa, the land of my struggles:
Your prisons have given me hope!
Your challenges made me truly human!
Your limitations are my opportunities!
This is my South Africa . . . Mine.

South Africa, the land of my death:
Look at the heroes of Sharpeville!
After Hector Peterson you'll never be the same again!
After Steve Biko a new era is bound to come!
For better and for worse this is my country . . . Mine.

South Africa, the land of my hopes:
Watch my huge wide dream!
Kiss my great dream come true!
Our cause has ultimately triumphed!
Truly this is my only country . . . Mine.

South Africa, the land of my everything:
My land by right, not privilege!
My country by birth, not default!
My ancestors are buried here, my descendants shall live here!
Who shall divorce me from my land, South Africa?
                        Mine.

Government gone crazy

There was once Saul, chosen of God:
   Born of small tribe of Benjamin,
   Small tribe, humble beginnings.
Elevated by the hand of God:
   Seated on the throne of power,
   A king among kings,
   To lead and serve his nation Israel:
   To rule in justice and in love,
   To care for the orphan and the widow,
   To offer shelter to the stranger,
Above all to serve the king of kings, Yahweh the Kingmaker.

There was once a Lucifer chosen of God:
   Full of self, drunk with pride,
   Futile coup against God he led.
Misled by thirst for power:
   He drew his sword against the Almighty,
   An evil angel among his evil crowd,
   To lead revolt against the Ancient of days:
   To promote evil against good,
   To establish injustice, not righteousness,
   To deny food to the hungry and water to the thirsty,
And above all to rob God of his godly rights.

In 1948 a government was born:
   Born of the Voortrekker tribe,
   Of Dutch descent, of French Huguenots:
Elevated by the barrel of the gun,
   Entered into covenant with the god of self,
   A bloodthirsty god, god of Blood river:
   In God's name to maim and kill,
   In his name to rob and misrule,
   To crush the soulless black kaffir race,
   In hewing wood and drawing water,
Above all to serve Sem and Japhet the white tribe.

Strange twins apartheid and reform:
   Born of barren parents, bankruptcy of mind,
   Public safety act, insecurity for public at large:
1967 Terrorism Act terror for all,
1982 Internal Security Act turmoil for all:

Ever heard laws sing like a choir?
Rock 'n roll apartheid music of oppression:
Legislate against blackness,
Detain and torture young and old,
Security's call: maim and kill:
Kill black ideas, hopes and dreams,
Above all, kill their desire to be like God and us.

State of emergency 1960 born of fear:
State of emergency 1985,
State of emergency 1986,
1987 Urgent State of emergency,
Ever heard the voice of truth?
Gospel music South African Broadcasting Corporation:
All are happy save communists,
All secure everywhere,
Situation under control,
Peace reigns countrywide,
Above all, white man, you are in control.

Take off your hats, honor the great patriot,
Johan Coetzee, greatest of police commissioners,
His mouthpiece the government gazette:
Law and Order, Baal and Asherah,
Campaign not for your beloved ones,
No projects to see them free,
Freedom not good for them,
Worship Internal Security Act 1982,
Shout not, call not for their release,
Above all take to heart Romans thirteen.

Not by telegram, pen and ink!
Disapproval not detention without trial,
Not by document, not by protest, pen and ink,
Freedom-poster, sticker and T-shirt all taboo,
Think not, speak not, act not, feel not:
Protest gatherings not for you:
Disgraced by government, dishonored by you,
Wisdom menu June 12 '86,
Security garment December 11 '86,
April 10 '87 washdown,
Above all glory to God from whom all governments come.

Defy Satan, defy tyranny

Long live prophet Samuel;
Long live Gad the prophet;
Long live prophet Nathan.
   David is man and not God,
   Yahweh is God and not man.
   Man's will within God's will,
   God's will be done!

Long live prophet Desmond;
Long live Allan the prophet;
Long live prophet Beyers.
   Botha is man and not Yahweh,
   Yahweh is God and not Coetzee.
   Pretoria subject to Heaven's will,
   Heaven's will be done!

Side by side with Isaiah, the prophet;
Hand in hand with fiery Jeremiah;
Eyeball to eyeball against evil forces.
   Apartheid is a state of emergency;
   God is state of life and truth.
   Coetzee is here and Coetzee shall go;
   Father's will here to stay!

Take after Amos, take after God;
Life to the dead Ezekiel style;
Justice to all Micah's way.
   Power and death, twins of sorrow,
   Verwoerd Vorster one in sin, one in death.
   In Apartheid river roam crocodiles of destruction,
   Creator's will is the river of life!

Defy Satan lovers of justice;
Reject tyranny, democrats of South Africa;
Pull down the walls of Jericho freedom fighters.
   Guns shoot but guts will win,
   Teargas is smoke; hope is freedom.
   They dictate policy; we dictate the future.
   He's the Alpha and Omega; we in between!

Parliament shall speak; the world shall be deaf;
Tutu shall whisper and all shall listen;

The flock shall follow; they know the shepherd's voice.
    Legislative power to Cape Town,
    Judicial power to Bloemfontein,
    Executive power to Pretoria,
    All power to the Almighty.
        Power!
        Glory!
        Kingdom!
        Amen.
        Not yet!

Defy Satan, Tutu, the Daniel way;
Assail Pharaoh Boesak, the Meshach way;
Shake Dagon Naude, the Shadrach way.
    Nebuchadnezzar is powerful, not immortal;
    Belshazzar is arrogant, but shall rot.
    Tyrants fall; prophets stand,
    God be god; Botha be botha.
        Justice!
        Freedom!
        Love!
        Amen!

Rabbi Franklin, may you close with a word of prayer?
Shout loud, Bishop Hurley;
Blow the trumpet, Frank Chikane;
Courage and faith, Francois Bill.
    May the grace of our Lord Jesus Christ,
    the love of God our father, and
    the fellowship of the Holy Spirit our comforter,
    be with us all. A—men!

Permanent Tourists

April 6, 1652.
Dromedaris, Reyger, and De Goede Hoop docked at the Cape,
"Hundreds" marched out to bask in "our" sun:
A small garden in 1652,
An orchard half-way between East and West,
Said the Dutch East India Company.

It was night and it was day, the second phase.
Shout for joy descendants of Sem:
Your gardens shall be your farms,
From orchards a country shall be born,
Another Holland at Africa's toe,
Said the Dutch East India Company.

And it was night and it was day, third stage.
Give way descendants of Ham:
Your stock and land belong to our god;
Milk and honey not meant for you,
Unless you die you'll draw our water and chop our wood,
Said the Dutch East India Company.

And it was night and it was day, the fourth day.
Brittania rules the waves; Brittania rules the Cape:
Wake up sons and daughters of Israel;
Leave Egypt in the great trek;
Free State, Transvaal and Natal shall I give to you,
Said the prophet Piet Retief.

And it was night and it was day, the fifth phase.
Wake up daughters and sons of Africa:
Two bulls for one knife no more;
Beggars cannot be choosers;
Guests do not accommodate their hosts,
Said the spirit of freedom!

And it was day and it was night, 1948.
Stand up Broederbond; wake up Afrikaner giant:
The horse of power is here for you,
Jan Smuts shall walk; you take the saddle,
Gallop in the tested desert of divide and rule,
Said the united volk, nationalist powerbase.

And it was day and it was night, the darkest Sabbath.
Praise the Lord Nederduits Gereformeerde Kerk:
Fast and feast Hervormde Kerk,
Burn incense Gereformeerde Kerk,
Sit on their backs; the White Sabbath is here,
Said the spirit of self-deceit.

The night came; the night went, Blacks' day:
Stand up, stand up, Bambata,
Shake off the yoke Hintsa,
Tshaka and Sekhukhuni will take your side;
Makhado shall hold the north;
Said the voice of freedom:
    Birth to Mandela!
    Birth to Biko!
    Birth to People's power!
    Amandla!
    Ngawethu!
United Democratic Republic of South Africa.

You tried to isolate me: November 21-22, 1986

Looked helpless—
In the middle of the night you came—
With police from station—
Soldiers from borders—
You were many and I and family alone—
What could I have done?

Friends came and turned back—
Pastors stopped at the gate—
Doctors to offer help detained—
Children cried and granny groaned—
You were many and I alone—
What could I have done?

You were all armed and I not—
All angry and I in fear—
Ready to shoot and I helpless—
Dressed in treacherous dress and voice of deceit—
You were many and I alone—
What could I have done?

Telephone calls in the bedroom we managed—
Every key tried and failed—
A failure in the lock was a blessing—
The front door banged on and broken—
You were many and I alone—
What could I have done?

From eleven at night till half past six in the morning—
I could not sleep and rest—
You took me to the dungeon dark and dull—
"This time we'll close your mouth once and for all"—
You were many and I alone—
What could I have done?

Arms and ammunition I have not—
Testaments old and new I have—
Justice and truth like Amos I proclaim—
Apartheid is false; Pretoria is wrong—
You were many and I alone—
What could I have done?

The
government
　is
　not
　required
　to
　respond
　to
anti-government
　propaganda—Period.

Thank God Tshenu is back

He does not believe in empty words.
He sees no good in empty fellowhship.
He believes in Christ incarnate:
   Lover of outcasts,
   Healer of the sick,
   Friend of children,
   Faith incarnate.

Happy to be back with wife and children,
He enjoys his wife's love;
He loves his kids—two daughters and a son:
   Liberator of prisoners,
   Feeder of the hungry,
   Thirst quencher of the thirsty,
   Through Christ the incarnate.

Day and night the children asked,
Twenty-four hours a day we wept and cried,
Shall we trust Christ the incarnate?
   Shall they kill him mummy?
   Are they going to beat him again?
   Will they arrest us too?
   Police power, Satan incarnate.

God of miracles, will you bring him back?
But why Almighty allow this to happen?
What crime and what wrong, O God?
   His son knew where he was,
   His daughters loved him all the same,
   Their song and prayer from little lips,
   Pulled tears off Christ,the incarnate.

Thank God Tshenu is free;
Praise God he roams the larger prison;
Thank God he can again prophesy.
   No conversation with himself anymore,
   No more talking to the walls,
   No more company of evil captors,
   Safe now in the company of Christ, the incarnate.

Detain a dog in solitary confinement,
Keep a baboon for a month under similar conditions,

They shall not live for want of freedom.
   Intimidation his daily bread,
   Death threats by captain and colonel,
   Confessions born of coercion,
   Till saved by Christ, the incarnate.

Will the police commissioner take like medicine?
Dare the brigadier taste the pill?
Try the tormentors at the whip's end:
   Rivers of lies shall come down in flood;
   In half a month they will lose half their weight.
   The merciless shall scream for mercy;
   They'll plead with Jesus, the incarnate.

Apartheid faith

Black and religious,
Black and Christian,
A member of the body,
Shareholder in the faith.
   Whose brother am I?

Bible in hand, song on the lips,
Pious, polite,
Faithful in the choir,
Earmarked for paradise.
   Whose sister am I?

Taught to sing songs of love and praise,
Baptism and Confirmation behind me,
Steeped in the pacifist tradition,
Willing to turn the other cheek.
   Whose product am I?

Fed on the Ten Commandments and the Creeds,
Tailored for heaven and not for earth,
Schooled to hate my own and admire the oppressor.
Man without stomach, naked without shame.
   Whose image am I?

They love not that pray with me,
Same Bible and same God,
Same origin and same destiny,
Same humanity, rainbow colors.
   Whose piece of art am I?

Sharing tradition, not the building,
Sharing faith, not sacraments,
Sharing Christianity, not Christ,
Loving love, not the neighbor.
   Whose body is this?

Who is my neighbor?

Who lives next door?
   Is it my fellow Jew?
   Is it my fellow Christian?
   Is it my fellow countryman?
   Is it my oppressor?
   Is it Christ?

Who robs me of my humanity?
   Is it   Satan?
   Is it   communism?
   Is it   atheism?
   Is it   capitalism?
   Is it the Dutch Reformed Church?

Who promotes social evils in black society?
   Is it the work of subversives?
   Is it the plot of agitators?
   Is it the prophecy of false prophets?
   Is it a matter of instigation?
   Is it Botha himself?

Who stripped blacks of their political rights?
   Is it Nelson Mandela the "terrorist?"
   Is it Bram Fisher the "communist?"
   Is it Joe Slovo the "marxist?"
   Is it Robert Sobukwe the black "racist?"
   Is it Malan, Verwoerd, Vorster and sons?

Who murdered blacks in their search for freedom?
   Was it Fidel Castro in Sharpeville?
   Was it Brezhnev in Soweto 1976?
   Did Samora Machel kill Steve Biko?
   Did Tambo kill Neil Aggett?
   Is it white murder?

On the Jericho Road

August 1947.
Down Black Avenue
From a black womb.
Into slavery.
Who will nurse my wounds?

Removals in June.
Resettled in winter.
Loss of stock and land.
Into poverty.
Who's that walking past my poverty?

Denied timely education.
School without facilities.
Force-fed Bantu education.
Into servitude.
Who's that walking past my ignorance?

First class in gutter education.
High schools far far away.
Away from school to child labor.
Into ten cents a day.
Who's that speaking in tongues past my starvation?

Wages reduced five cents a day.
Protest silenced by holy whip.
Police on side of robbers.
Add stripes to my wounded back.
Who's that Full Gospel cleric walking past injustice?

Louis Trichardt, St. Wolmarans Street.
Labor seventeen hours a day.
In the kitchen and in the garden.
Pigs and cows for eight cents a day.
Who's that preaching that man can live on the word alone?

Banged on the head.
Collapsed and convulsed.
December 19, 1965.
Into unemployment—dismissal.
Who's that adventist walking past because it's Sabbath day?

Locked up.
Isolated.
One thousand kilometers between cell and home.
Into hell.
Will he with the golden cross walk past my wounds?

Incarcerated.
Seventeen souls crowded into one cell.
Toilet water for thirst.
Into pig-world.
Will the bread prophet walk past the prison on his way to the palace?

Bundled up and handcuffed.
Undressed and dressed in leaves.
Stripped of health and hope.
Into despair and state of disrepair.
Who's that faith healer walking past the sick to doctor the healthy?

Back into the dungeon.
Death threats.
Hungry. Thirsty. Naked. Sick. Stranger. Prisoner.
Despair, death and will to Regina.
Will Bishop Anonymous walk past Lazarus in the grave?

Priests are busy.
Christians are not politicians.
Atheists care.
Communists love.
Brother Samaritan thank you for saving my life:
   In Christ.
   For Christ.

Here we stand!

Why probably?
    Possibly!
Why perhaps?
    Maybe!
Scholars fear to take a stand—
Theologians fear to take sides—
Politicians circle issues—
Every person for himself and God for us all.

Why neither yes nor no?
    Yes—no!
Why neither conservative nor progressive?
    Moderate!
Quick at tackling concepts—
Fast at challenging space—
Always slow to call a spade a spade—
One leg in hell one leg in paradise—
Every genius on a scholastic fence.

When we say God is one, there is no other.
When we speak of God's race, there's no sub-human race.
When we respect our parents, we are right.
When we condemn murder, we are right.
Either we are hot or we are cold.
    Warm?
Either we are boiling or we are freezing.

When we say people are equal, we are right.
When we call for equality of sexes, we are right.
When we condemn discrimination, we are right.
When we right wrong, we are right.
Either we are for or we are against.
    Fence-sitting?
Either we approve or disapprove.

When we say apartheid is heresy, we mean it.
When we call for its demise, we don't mean to reform it.
When we call for support we don't mean slogans.
When we say we shall win, we mean they shall lose.
Either we are winners or we are losers.
    Gambling?
Either we pay the price or remain slaves.

When we call for release of children,
We want to see them free.
When we say Uhuru to all,
We want freedom to all.
When we say injury to one,
We mean injury to all.
When we say black is beautiful,
We mean our noses are flat, some flattened.
Either we take a stand or fall.
    Investing?
Either we become ourselves or shadows of others.

When we say police are beasts,
We've heard them roar.
When we call them murderers,
We can take you to the graves.
When we call them torturers,
We have mutilated bodies.
When we call them Botha's dogs,
We've heard them bark at his call.
Either we call them by name or they'll never know themselves.
    Prodigals?
Either we say Amen or pray without an end.

We are not afraid of 1652.
We are not afraid of Van Riebeeck.
We are not afraid of white paint.
We are not afraid of the SADF.*
    We Africans through and through!
    Before them we were here!

---

*SADF: South African Defense Force.

Kids' questions are the toughest

It may be origin,
It may be destiny,
Or a bulging stomach,
Or an innocent question about the bouncing bed,
Kids' questions are the toughest.

Before they are born,
They kick from within.
When arriving,
They scream in the air.
Kids' questions are the toughest.

If mom sports a blue eye,
If she fails to smile,
Or dad fails to kiss as usual,
Or pats mom too hard on the back,
Kids' questions are the toughest.

You walk arm in arm in the garden,
Small one in between.
Then comes that incisive sting.
Dad will never beat mom, will he?
Kids' questions are the toughest.

One climbs your shoulder;
Another on your back,
From this one in your arm:
Do you love me more than you do them mom?
Kids' questions are the toughest.

An innocent woman visits you;
Your nestlings have never seen her before.
After sunset mom is not yet back.
Will she sleep on your bed dad? The 2½ year old asks.
Kids' questions are the toughest.

Mom comes home with a dress.
Dad surely has not bought this one.
An innocent friend comes by to greet.
Did another man buy this for you mom?
Kids' questions are the toughest.

They go to the neighbor's home.
The room is filled with elderly women.
You are among friends, and your four year old pulls your skirts:
When will you make another little baby mom?
Kids' questions are the toughest.

Police grab you at the dead of night.
And beat you tot die nerwe waai.*
At home mom faces questions day and night.
Will they beat him mom?
Kids' questions are the toughest.

You have a friend.
Police grab him and kill him.
All your kids know him and ask,
Has God taken him to the clouds?
Kids' questions are the toughest.

A policeman leads your congregation.
Your kids know Satan is bad and God is good.
Are the police Satan dad?
Why does the congregational leader not free our father mom?
Kids' questions are the toughest.

You are back home and about to settle down.
They crowd you with ball-size eyes:
Did they beat you dad?
Did you cry?
When will they come again?
Kids' questions are tougher than security police questions!

---
*beat to pieces.

Informer

He is salesman.
He sells everything.
He sells for commission:

    He sold his own soul.
    He sold his brother.
    Hard cash for his neighbor,
    A pat on the back,
    For his daughter's soul.

A salesman,
He sells every day.
He sells to kill:

    He sold him for life.
    He sold her to hang.
    Ten rand for a banning order,
    A bonus in mid-year,
    For his mother's soul.

A general dealer,
He sells everybody.
He sells for gain:

    He sold his bishop.
    He sold his teacher.
    Krugerrand for his doctor,
    A step up the ladder,
    For his senior's soul.

An agent-provocateur,
He sells hot ideas.
He sells for self:

    He sold Gonville his ideas.
    He sold me his political music.
    An increase for his wife,
    A trip abroad,
    For his son's soul.

He is a salesbeast.
He sold his own soul.
Selling his birthright for pottage,
He is a soulless soul.

Stooge

If he smiles,
Another is smiling.

If he walks,
His master is walking.

If he is silent,
His god is dumb.

His master is full.
His hungry stomach is satisfied.

His baas is rich.
His starving people have plenty.

"Are you happy?"
"Master, am I happy?"
"Yes, you are."
"Yes, I am."

"Apartheid is good."
"Yes, master apartheid is the solution."
"Apartheid is outdated and dead."
"Yes, master we've been against apartheid all along."

"I am for Gerrie Coetzee."
"I am against Tate, master."
"We've lost. Gerrie is beaten."
"We've won. Tate has won. We've lost. Gerrie is beaten."

If he passes a law,
It's Pretoria's shade.

If Pretoria's against you,
He wars against you.

When his master dies,
He ceases to breathe.

Trees

You see, some live in a row.
  You know, some stand alone.
    Yet, no one is alone.
      Yet, none is lonely.
        They are together,
          A family,
            Like my family tree.

You see, some are big.
  You know, some are tall.
    Yet, no one is isolated.
      Yet, none are dwarfed.
        They are all trees,
          All fauna,
            Like my family tree.

You chop one, you threaten them all.
  You dig around one, you hurt others' roots.
    One lives for the other.
      One falls on others for support.
        They are neighbors.
          All colors,
            Like my family tree.

You see these yellow flowers.
  You see the pink blossom.
    You see the red and white.
      You see the black and cream.
        They are all beauty,
          For all eyes,
            Like my family tree.

Yet, we cannot enjoy the shade.

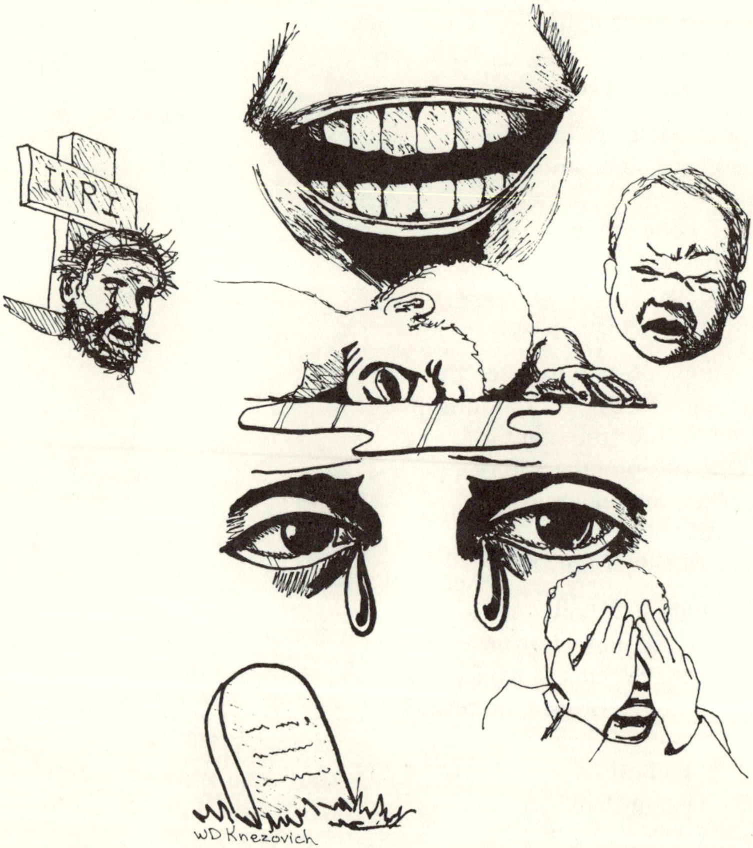
INRI
wD Knezovich

Crying is for men

Men can cry
Males have tears
Men should weep
Males are human
Men are children
I love to cry
Like a child
I hate to laugh
I am not guilty
For shedding tears
Unless you say
I made myself
Put the blame
If you wish
Before the one
Who wept
Before the grave
Where Lazarus slept
All great men cry
Calvin cried
My father cried
Luther cried
Luthuli cried
All good men cry
Christ cried: Eli, Eli, lama sabachtani?
Satan laughs
Always laughing
Has no feelings
For the poor
For the hungry
For the bereaved
Crying is only for men
And they are few.

If I were a god

I would not be good
I would not do well
I would mess up the world
I would not be colorless
I would not love everybody
I would have long resigned
Left
Man
to
his
own
devices
for
I
would
not
be
God.

I love my country so much . . . .

that I was born below the mountain,
was raised among the trees,
eating muladza[1] every morning,
drinking mabundu[2] in the field,
sharing milk with my father's calves
which are no more.

that in my father's wheelbarrow,
mounted on cow dry dung,
a fig in every little hand,
two oranges bulging in my dirty innocent pockets,
we drove to his orchard-garden
which is no more.

that I carved fertile ground behind the plough,
opening wide smiles on the face of the earth,
observing the first commandment after the fall,
to eat no meal unspiced by sweat,
in these fertile fields fit for gods
which are no more.

that I learned with every removal,
from up there to down here,
vertical mobility face down,
facing loss with faces of ghosts,
valuables falling through our fingers
which is the case still.

that full of youthful passion I joined Vesa,[3]
later in Saso[4] became myself,
in BPC[5] fought for my freedom,
till today in His collar,
calling for justice denied to my own,
which we shall surely get.

---

[1] left over porridge
[2] fermented non-alcoholic drink
[3] Venda Students Association
[4] South African Students Association
[5] Black Peoples' Convention

Botha you are not alone

Botha
was right
when he said
South Africa is not alone
In practicing apartheid in the world.

Thatcher was definitely wrong
When she claimed that Britain
Is non-racial all the way
For if it were so
Why would she
be as white as snow?

Botha
told the truth
when he challenged
Any white nation on the globe
To put blackie on top at the helm.

Reagan was right when he did not
say what we all know but cannot tell
That sanctions will hurt
not only apartheid and blacks
But over and above all
Whites.

Botha
knew the trick
When he defied the world
That despite their tough talk
Western nations would never now or ever
Raise their finger against kith and kin.

Botha
You are the top
of an iceberg
of a world-wide disease of racism.

In hell all are equal

Same temperature
   every corner.

Leaping flames
   everywhere.

Redhot screams
   by everyone.

Gnashing of teeth
   by every adult.

Bumping of gums
   by infant and toothless.

Hoarse pleas
   by every thirsty throat.

Babel of languages
   from every nation.

Loss of life
   with every breath.

Calling for mercy
   from down below.

Recanting apartheid
   from every whitened lip.

Send Steve Biko from paradise
   to every white mansion.

They are all equal!

All is equal!

Equal opportunity to all!

Age is no criterion!

Stellenbosch wine is missing here!

English and Afrikaans are not official!

Satan is fair to all races!

Chances in purgatory are nil!

Why not repent now?

Listen to prophets among you!

In hell all racists are equal.

The Lord is my shepherd
Psalm 23 in Pietermaritzburg and Howick
March 13–June 4, 1977

The Lord is my shepherd,
I shall not buckle.
He rests me in the land of freedom,
I drink from his cup of liberty.
Even when I wander in the valley of torture,
I shall fear no human beasts,
He shall fight my fight.
His angels and his visions,
Guide me through brutal interrogations.
He gives me life in the hands of murderers,
Giving me a crown for a victory his own.
I shall live among saints in my father's house,
Forever beyond the reach of human beasts!

The Lord is my shepherd
Psalm 23 Second Incarceration
October 21, 1977, to January 21, 1978

The Lord is my God,
I shall not serve idols.
He supports me in the land of oppression,
He steels my soul when I drink toilet water.
When I'm moved from Sibasa to Louis Trichardt,
I shall fear no warders,
In Pietersburg prison He shall break the lion's teeth.
His word and His spirit,
Inspire me when deflated by depression.
He gives me hope in the kingdom of despair,
A lease of new life in the land of death.
My soul is preserved for a free South Africa,
Forever free from the race epidemic!

The Lord is my shepherd
Psalm 23 from the bottom of hell
November 18, 1981, to June 1, 1982

The Lord is my government,
I shall never bow to apartheid.
He rescues my soul from Masisi,
Like Lazarus I'm raised from the grave.
When broken and left naked,
I shall not tremble at the wounds.
When man seals my fate behind the curtain,
With the ink of his son's blood in his mighty hand,
He opens a new page in my life.
He brings me friends from far and near,
Letters from good Samaritans here and everywhere.
I shall walk tall and free,
Forever in Jesus' name.

The Lord is my shepherd
Psalm 23 from the land of manna and quail
November 21, 1986–January 30, 1987

The Lord is my advocate,
I shall never be guilty.
He destroys their every plot.
He removes their traps before my feet.
Besieged and hounded by night,
I shall not give in without a fight.
When Captain Above-the-law threatens to close my
Mouth once and for all,
Before me unrolls the red carpet of abundant life.
He opens holes on the warrant of arrest,
Letting food in and letters out.
They may win many battles now;
The last one will be God's and ours.

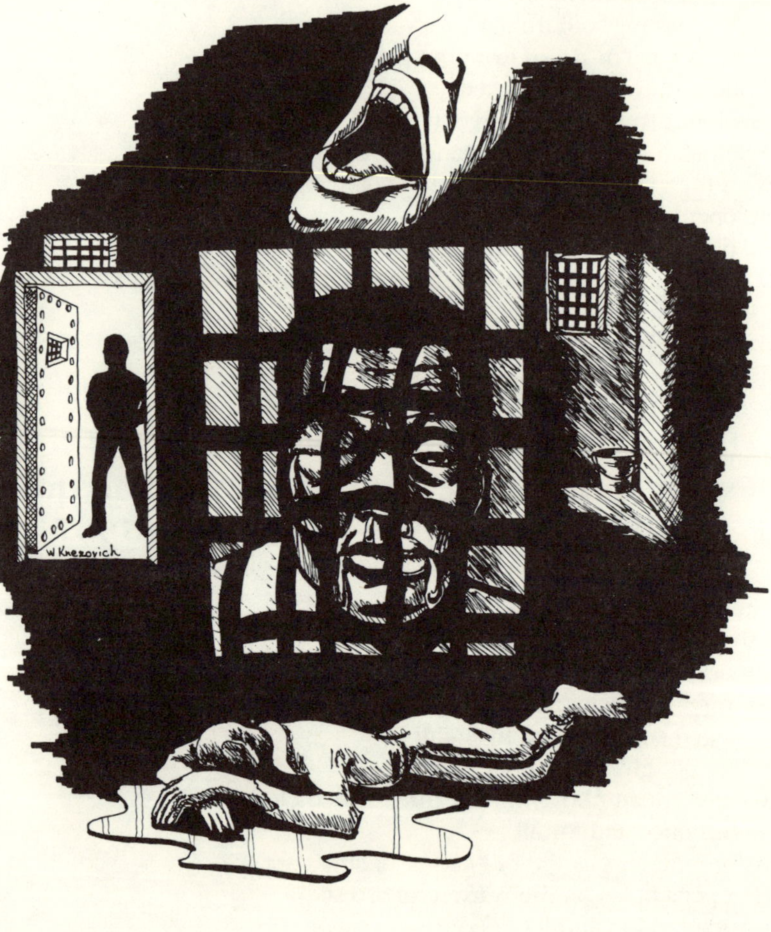
W Knezovich

This place is dirty

It is small.
It is square.
This place is dirty.

A bucket for a toilet.
Water in the bucket.
This place is dirty.

Small window at the back.
Another far above the door.
This place is dirty.

A leaking roof.
Wet, smelling blankets.
This place is dirty.

Blackened, tasteless coffee.
Maize grains with worms.
This place is dirty.

Worms in every bite.
Phutu[1] and phuzamandla.[2]
This place is dirty.

A peep hole on the door.
Blanket dust on the floor.
This place is dirty.

Light controlled from outside.
On and off at Satan's whim.
This place is dirty.

Waking up at siren's call.
Blankets folded in a heap.
This place is dirty.

Sitting alone in a lonely cell.
Admiring beauty in the ugly walls.
This place is dirty.

---

[1] Hard crumbling porridge
[2] Energy drink

Here ghosts have footsteps,
Footsteps that leave no prints.
This place is dirty.

Skik. Skik. Skik.
Bucket. Bucket. Bucket.
This place is dirty.

Toilet paper on the floor.
Not enough for infant's arse.
This place is dirty.

No access to lawyer and family.
No access to reason.
This place is dirty.

You sing at a price.
You labor for no wage.
This place is dirty.

No changing clothes.
No soap and face cloth.
This place is dirty.

You speak to yourself.
You preach to yourself.
This place is dirty.

You sit on nothing.
You walk to nowhere.
This place is ugly.

You hear screams by night.
You see naked people by day.
This place is ugly.

Some are handcuffed in ice cold water.
Women in tattered clothes.
This place is ugly.

Preaching loudly is a crime.
Greeting is treason.
This place is ugly.

Don't sleep during the day.
Don't look innocent without a crime.
This place is ugly.

Exercise is a privilege.
Shower if you are lucky.
This place is ugly.

Humanity is as scarce as gold.
Here angels fear to tread.
This place is ugly.

Blankets and clothes are thrown apart,
Left scattered without explanation.
This place is ugly.

If you are sick,
You'll curse your god.
This place is ugly.

If you love company,
You'll love yourself.
This place is ugly.

If you count hours,
You'll die before you count days.
This place is ugly.

If you love meat,
You'll eat your own flesh.
This place is ugly.

If you love arithmetic,
You'll count your toes.
This place is ugly.

If you are afraid,
You'll fear fear.
This place is ugly.

If you want interrogation,
You are kept unquestioned.
This place is dirty.

If you are tired of questions,
The interrogation continues.
This place is dirty.

When you have answers,
You are not asked.
This place is dirty.

When you do not know,
You must know.
This place is dirty.

When you feel pain,
You must not cry.
This place is dirty.

When you fail to cry,
You are cheeky.
This place is dirty.

When you confess,
It's all rubbish.
This place is dirty.

When you vomit nonsense,
Peace prevails.
This place is dirty.

When you are tired,
You must not rest.
This place is dirty.

When you are hungry,
There's no food.
This place is ugly.

When you faint,
You are faking.
This place is ugly.

You want to sit,
They make you stand.
This place is ugly.

Now you want to stand,
But you must sit.
This place is ugly.

You want to say no;
They want yes.
This place is ugly.

You are ready with your yes;
They are ready for your no.
This place is ugly.

Now you are a gentleman;
Next minute you are baboon.
This place is ugly.

You get a smile,
Followed by a punch.
This place is ugly.

One of them is black;
But behaves white every way.
This place is ugly.

You must speak Afrikaans,
Good Afrikaans means you think you are white.
This place is dirty.

You were there when you were not there;
When you were there you were absent.
This place is dirty.

You meant what you did not say;
You said what you did not mean.
This place is dirty.

You must worship the god you don't believe;
You must believe without faith.
This place is ugly.

Here God is called Satan;
Sour is sweet.
This place is ugly.

You are wrong when you are right;
You are equal when you are slave.
This place is ugly.

You want to talk,
But you must write.
This place is ugly.

You write,
And your statement is shredded.
This place is ugly.

When unsympathetic magistrates come,
A smile through your tears.
This place is ugly.

Any problems?
Before you say yes he's out of sight.
This place is ugly.

You lie bloodied and dying,
And get pills for the flu and venereal disease.
This place is ugly.

Upside down,
You see the land from above.
This place is ugly.

Handcuffed and suspended on a stick between two tables,
You cackle like a hen.
This place is ugly.

Barefoot and naked,
You stand on blunt nails.
This place is ugly.

Long hair and long beard,
Are all lost in a violent shave.
This place is bad.

Frog jumping for heavyweights,
Pressups without limit.
This place is bad.

In the cold room,
You press button when you are ready to tell the "truth."
This place is bad.

All you know about communism is the word itself;
Here you are communism yourself.
This place is bad.

If by accident your lawyer and bishop see you,
There's nothing that they can do.
This place is bad.

They mock your call,
And insult the area below the belt.
This place is dirty.

You miss the love,
And embrace of your wife.
This place is ugly.

Here they call a spade a spade,
Black is Kaffir and white is Baas.
This place is ugly.

It is here that fools are kings,
And rule the wise.
This place is ugly.

Here post graduates,
Receive instruction from grade two professors.
This place is ugly.

There's no choice here,
You may be alone or seventeen in a small cell.
This place is ugly.

They are against violence from all that is black;
For violence to preserve all that is white.
This place is bad.

If we have to choose between power-sharing and wiping you out;
None of you will remain.
This place is ugly.

Roof corrugated iron,
Walls zinc all around.
This place is ugly.

On your head against the wall,
White punches and kicks land from above and below.
There's death here.

Head banged against the wall,
Thrown into the air to fall on the concrete floor below.
There's death here.

Karate and judo chops and kicks,
Total onslaught.
There's death here.

Hit with sticks and chairs,
Assailed by muscular men.
There's death here.

Bloodied nose, mouth and knee,
Bruised below, above and everywhere.
There's death here.

If you are alive by tomorrow,
Then we do not know our job.
There's death here.

Behind closed doors and curtains drawn,
Captain R and Sergeant M lead the team.
There's death here.

Naked and handcuffed behind the back,
Nobody leaves this room alive unless he says and does the master's will.
There's death here.

By close of day,
Everything has gone according to plan.
There's death here.

Ankles, wrists, knees, eyes, ears, head, nose and ribs,
Have had their share of pain.
There's death here.

You call to God to take your life;
You call on Satan to exercise mercy.
This place is dirty.

You hate life;
And love to die.
This place is ugly.

You look for God,
And find none.
This place is ugly.

You lose faith,
And find God.
This place is funny.

You tell lies to uphold the truth;
You withhold the truth to frustrate liars.
This place is funny.

You want to die.
They give you food.
This place is dirty.

You decide to die.
They let you live.
GOD IS STILL IN CHARGE.

Farewell to innocence

Farewell to non-violence;
Innocence, I'll never meet you again.
Until the work is done,
When apartheid is undone.
Then I'll be innocent again,
When violence is needed no more.
   Don't push me too far!

Forward Umkonto we sizwe.[1]
Peace and I will never walk hand in hand.
Until the boers are crushed,
When discrimination is history.
Then I'll love again,
When hatred is needed no more.
   Don't push me too far!

Crush the SADF[2] and security forces;
Life is not precious any more.
Until the boers respect our lives,
When minority rule is paralyzed.
Then I will forgive again,
When anger is required no more.
   Don't push me too far!

Slaughter them all wholesale;
Mow them down child and all.
Until their pride is smashed,
When their ego is deflated.
Then I'll preach salvation again,
When hell has cleansed racist hearts.
   Don't push God too far!

---

[1] Spear of the Nation, the armed wing of the African National Congress.
[2] South African Defense Force.

I am not a politician

Yesterday I wanted all these white ants killed.
Today I want them all saved.
They have to die for they killed our people,
Without death we are without freedom.

They must live because Christ died for them!

Last year I called them all devils,
Today I know some are angels.
They are devils for their behavior is evil.
Without throwing them into hell we'll never see heaven.

They'll repent because in Christ nothing is impossible!

Last week I called Botha an incorrigible racist.
Today I believe there's a silver lining in this racist cloud.
He is incorrigible for he never bends.
Without breaking him we'll never break our chains.

He'll change for he is now headed for Damascus!

Last month I invited all of you to war.
Today I believe in the way of peace.
War! War against the war-mongers.
Without war peace will never come.

God will change swords into ploughshares!

In my anger I opened floodgates of wrath.
Today I want to stem the tide.
Throw all these fascist racists into the ocean.
Unless they drown we'll never emerge.

Man's anger does not work the righteousness of God!

Were it the other way round...

Were Botha black
And his nose flat,
Were he black African
And his hair curled and thick,
Surely he would never
Have things his way.

Were we five millions
Against twenty-five million whites,
Were twenty-five thousand whites in jail
And ten thousand of their children behind bars,
Surely we would never
Have things our way.

Were Mandela in power
And Botha below his boot,
Were whites starving
and blacks overfed,
As Berliners never starved
So would never the whites.

Were we to be free tomorrow
And roles changed except for numbers,
To have LeGrange in Mabopane
and Luthuli in Lower Houghton,
Surely the West would move to remove the evil,
Not for whites, but for the sake of justice. Of course.

Were God black
And Satan white,
Were Christianity black
And Afrikanerdom white,
Whites would choose to settle in hell,
Among the volk away from life.

Sankambe the Sly

"I Sankambe.
See me as I am.
My eyes are open all day,
Because of fear."

I chase with the hounds,
And run with the hare.
Sleep during the day
And work at night.

My gods change every day,
What feeds me that I worship.
Whoever wins, that is my hero,
If he loses gone is my support.

I meet Satan and call him god.
I meet a slave and call him king.
My enemy is my friend.
Like a weather cock I depend on the winds.

I'll smile if you wish.
I'll stab your heart with friendly eyes.
My handshake might mow you down,
While you plant in me your total trust.

I detest apartheid as you do.
I hate change as my masters do.
I fight all who oppress my people.
Oppressors cannot succeed without me.

When change comes I'll change first.
If it does not last I'll change fast.
Sankambe is my name,
I don't even trust myself.

There is nothing for nothing: Dialogue between a pig and a hen

Knock-knock. Knock-knock.
Who is there?
Hen.
Come in, Mrs. Hen.
Good morning, Mr. Pig.
Good morning (Mr. Pig moves to kiss Mrs. Hen). No, Mr. Pig. Kisses will not do.
Good morning, Mrs. Hen. You have an unusual sparkle of beauty and health today. What happened?
Nothing, Mr. Pig.
Something happened, Mrs. Hen. What did you do for them? There's nothing for nothing in this world.
Now I understand, Mr. Pig. I give them two eggs a day. They feed me four times a day. That's the deal. You are overweight, Mr. Pig. What happened?
I am very well fed these days, Mrs. Hen.
There's nothing for nothing in this world, Mr. Pig.
I give them commitment, Mrs. Hen. You give them involvement.
What is the difference, Mr. Pig?
Simple, Mrs. Hen. You give eggs and you are still around. When my time comes they'll want pork, ham and bacon. Perhaps chitlings. After they are finished with me you will pick my bones.
I am also committed, Mr. Pig. You are not doing any better.
You can't do better than I, Mrs. Hen.
I can, Mr. Pig.
Mrs. Hen (Mr. Pig grabs her wings and all) before I meet my commitments I'll let you have a taste of what commitment is all about: Chew. Chew. Swallow. Digest. Now I wait my turn.

Sermon on Table Mountain

Blessed are the poor in apartheid votes,
for theirs is the non-racial future.

Blessed are those who mourn in Pollsmoor,
for freedom shall wipe away their tears.

Blessed are gentle prisoners in Robben Island,
for their isolation shall bring many together.

Blessed are those who hunger and thirst for justice,
for they will heal our broken nation.

Blessed are those who show mercy to apartheid victims,
for they give hope to many.

Blessed are those whose hearts are purified of racism,
for racists have no abode in the father's house.

Blessed are the freedom fighters,
for they will bring peace to all.

Blessed are the life prisoners,
those persecuted for their color,
for the kingdom of democracy is theirs.

Blessed are you when racists insult you,
And ban you,
And call you all names,
On account of your love for justice,

Jump up and shout amandla,
for your day of freedom is near,
for so racists persecuted Mugabe and Kaunda before you.

You are the liberators of the land;
if liberators sell out,
who will rehabilitate them?
They are puppets,
good for the garbage bin,
and ridiculed by their own people.

You are freedom signs for the oppressed.
Freedom fighters cannot be trounced.

Nor do democrats light the flame
And smother it under the ego;

they hoist it like a flag,
calling on the oppressed to stand up.

Let your freedom zeal dwarf all oppression,
So that the downtrodden may see the path to Uhuru;
And glorify God and his freedom children.

Do not think that freedom destroys law and order;
It does not destabilize;
it creates justice and peace.

Until apartheid and racism pass away,
not the youngest child will give up the struggle,
not until the evil is uprooted trunk, root and all.

Whoever robs one of these blacks the least of their human rights,
And teaches that apartheid is from God,
he shall be called heretic in the kingdom of God.
Whoever respects these rights and promotes them,
he shall be called liberator in the kingdom of God.

Unless your non-racialism surpasses that of Hitler and Verwoerd,
You are no material for eternal life.

You heard the immorality act say:
You shall not love across the color bar,
Whoever so loves falls foul of the law.

But I say to you:
If you frown at your neighbor's color,
You frown at his maker.
If you shout kaffir to your compatriot,
You roll his maker in the mud.
If you expose his mind to bantu education,
You insult his maker's brain.

If you are kneeling for sacraments in the kerk,*
And remember that Mandela is still in prison,
turn your back on the chalice.
First open the prison door,
reconcile yourself to Winnie, his wife,
then go back and recite Ons vader in die hemel.**

---

*Kerk = church.
**Our Father who art in heaven.

Make friends with the oppressed while still on the way to freedom,
Lest you curse your color on freedom day,
And reap the fruits of the internal security act,
drinking to the last poison drop from the apartheid cup.

You heard the prohibition of the mixed marriages act say:
In one bed black and white is adultery,
even if blessed by pope.
But I say to you:
Every dominie taking a black nanny to Lesotho,
to impose his holiness upon her black chastity,
his throne is not among the saints.

And if the right wing pulls you to Waterberg,
tear it out and throw away the malignant tumor;
it is better for a few racists to commit suicide,
than for the whole of Afrikanerdom to be thrown into hell.

If the ultra wing pulls you to Morass-stad,
Cut Marais out and right the wrong,
it is better to sacrifice cheap unity for eternal life,
than plunge into hell hand in hand.

You heard influx control say:
Whoever sends back to the homeland an exhausted bantu,
Let the bantu receive a certificate of "out of order."

But I say to you:
Whoever exploits my children,
And calls them expendable labor,
reduces them to animals.
And whoever marries this evil,
marries my wrath.

At Blood river you heard it said:
God's covenants are not enough;
Afrikaner make your own.

But I say to you:
Create no racist covenants,
either at the Voortrekker monument,
or at Verwoerd's tomb,
for all these are God's places of justice,
God's shrines of equality.

Do not swear by "die stem,"*
for it is the anthem of hate;
or by the Republic,
for it is a symbol of exclusion;
nor by your head,
for you are heading for trouble.

Let your development be development,
not parallel development;
Let your white be white.
God did not create Adam and honorary Adam.
All these qualifications racist minds produce.

You have heard it said:
"Dit sal die dag wees;"
Kaffir will know his place.

But I say to you:
Walk not into racial slogans.
When you are incited against God,
Let the agitator jump first into the ring.
Your cheeks are no punching bag.

And whoever shall force you back to the homeland,
force him back to Holland too.

Give trouble to those who ask for it,
And do not turn away until they ask for mercy.

You heard it said that:
You shall love only whites
And hate blacks.

But I say to you:
Love blacks too.

And you blacks pray for those who persecute you,
So that you may live as freely as your father,
to share his graces:
basking in his colorless sun,
his colorless rain drenching the colorful earth.

For if you love within your race,
What inbreeding is that?
Does Satan not love himself?

---

*National Anthem for whites.

And if you greet your sisters only,
How do you better the record of whitehead?
Did the Nazis not do better?

Christian sisters,
Christian brothers,
Muslims and Hindus,
Buddhists and traditionalists,
   Atheists
   Neutralists
You heard it said:
Condemn apartheid and trade with it,
Call for its end and veto resolutions to end it;
Condemn white violence and black resistance,
Deny blacks support and condemn those who offer it:
   Move in circles till you "become a wheel"
   Wallow in mud till you become a pig,
   Repeat a lie till it's iced with truth,
   Vilify the truth till it sounds like a lie,
   Call Satan god till he speaks in tongues,
   Call heaven hell till flames leap on angels' wings:
     "If only Christian nations were nations of Christians"
     If faith were not only a domesticated mamba,
     It would bite and evil would perish.

On that day

   The deaf shall hear freedom news
   The dumb shall not cease in their newfound speech
   The ugly shall become models
   Baboons shall walk on twos
   In the land of Uhuru

   Bones shall come together
   Skeletons hand in hand
   Music of freedom oozing from the upper jaw
   Sharpeville straight on their feet
   Free from pass and curse

Gonna reap what you sow

Hating me,
You hate yourself.
Holding my hand,
You strengthen yours.

Despise your mother
And unfold the curse.
Unlearn the past
And strengthen the future.

Pushing me,
You trip yourself.
Propping me up,
Together we stand.

Belittle God,
And soon worship a stone.
Recant yourself
And live for others.

Oppressing me,
You bend your back.
If you let go,
You'll be as vertical as the blue gum tree.

Make people beasts,
And live in a game park.
"Your freedom ends,
Where my nose begins."

Let me be,
And you'll be.
Between his image and his will,
We live in ghettos of our choice.

What's ability without opportunity?

What's a man,
if nobody calls you sir?

What's a farmer,
without a farm?

What's a homeland,
when you own no home?

What's peace,
in a land torn apart?

He's not a husband
without a wife.

She's not a widow
whose husband lives.

What's a black president
who is controlled by the whites?

What's dangerous about the mamba,
caged in a zoo?

What's a black mayor,
when the city's laws are all white?

What's a doctorate,
where color is the highest grade?

What's wrong with a tail,
if it's not a tell-tale of one's origins?

If wrong is righted,
and right is wronged,

Whose wrong is right,
whose right is wrong?

With no opportunities on earth,
the sky is the beginning, the earth the limit.

In a land where speech is crime,
the dumb will always be right.

I saw a millionaire,
eating shrimp on the curb.

A white pauper got five bucks from him
and ate among the kings.

I saw thousands moved against their will,
in the name of their own good.

If prisoners were as happy as warders believe,
then all warders would lose their jobs.

A boxer alone in the ring,
landing punches against the wind, does he earn a crown?

I know 25 million people in their land,
whose citizenship is in other lands.

"If the desire to kill and the opportunity never coincided,"
would anyone ever be charged for murder?

Thank God I've never had both.

Same—Same—Same everywhere!

If they call you bantu
   know you are black.

If they call you native,
   know there are no white natives.

If they call you non-white,
   the message is clear.

If you are british and black and they call you non-european,
   remember your roots.

If they call you third world,
   first and second class are reserved for others.

If you come to customs and all go unsearched except you,
   blame not fate, but the maker above.

If they call you terrorist in your search for freedom,
   remember that freedom fights and civil wars are for white alone.

If in self defense you bite his white penis, black lady,
   be sure to face charges of obstruction to self expression.

If you sit and all vacate their seats,
   remember that Hitler was not without friends.

If millions suffer and thousands die and the world whispers disapproval,
   you can be sure victims are black.

If victims cry and cocks crow,
   remember the one whose cry is colored by love.
      In him all people are the same everywhere.

Hit harder

I shall pat him on the back,
who kicks me at the back:
                            hard kick.
                            harder pat.

I shall offer her tea in a golden cup,
who gives me tea in a tin:
                            insulting love.
                            loving care.

I shall smile at them,
 that frown on me:
                            disgraceful mask,
                            enchanting smile.

I shall protect their lives,
that murder me:
                            bloodthirsty beasts,
                            saving hand.

I shall tell the truth to
those who are allergic to it:
                            lovers of death.
                            passionate for life.

I shall feed them eggs,
that feed me worms:
                            soiling the soul,
                            cleansing the mind.

I shall talk to them,
that shout at me:
                            tools of coercion
                            instrument of persuasion.

I shall love them hard,
that love to hate me:
                            addicted to hate,
                            for God so loved the world.

Ike

He
lived,
He
laughed,
He
loved,
And
died.

Isaac my friend. Tshifhiwa my colleague. Ike wahaMuofhe!
He was
    young,
He was
    fresh,
He was
    bold,
He was
    visionary.

He was taken. He was interrogated. We shall never know!
What he told,
    voluntarily.
What he said,
    pressured.
What he did,
    smiling.
What he did,
    tearfully.

He was b . . . . . . He was s . . . . . . God knows that . . . . !
He lost pints of blood,
    injured in the truck?
Injured kidneys,
      in the scuffle?
His scrotum subjected to,
      a hard fall?
Extensive lacerations all over,
        escape attempt?

He was conveyed. Into the cell. Was he alive?
I played with him
I fished with him.

I worked with him.
I married him.

Isaac. Tshifhiwa. Ike. Muofhe. Innocent. Smiling!
Lilian is a widow.
Mulanga is an orphan.
Mother less one son.
Freedom less one peaceful soldier.

Ike? Not Ike. Ike? Yes, Ike! I must be dreaming!
I saw his widow.
I saw *Mulanga** his daughter.
I missed his coffin.
Walked half-way the path he trod.

He lived. He laughed. He loved. He died. Yet he shall live!
In his
    grave
On his
    tombstone
In our minds
    ours
In his
    sleep
    freedom is
    AWAKE.

Isaac my friend. Tshifhiwa my brother. Charming Ike.

Doctors know he was hurt,
  by whom unknown.
The Bench knows it's not suicide "this time,"
  but nobody is to blame.
The dead is dumb;
  he is guilty.
The guilty speak;
  they are free.

R.I.P. Ike. When God shall open his mouth . . . . . . Cans of worms . . . . !

---

*Mulanga means Covenant in Venda.

Zion songs in foreign lands

In London.
Cold feet without socks.
Dad, it's he at the door!
Do you know him?
Yes, dad, I do!
Are you sure?
Down.
Down.
Down.

Ha! Ha! Ha! Ha! Come in my friend!
Ghost at Wilmington Square.
That's me at the door.
Am I dreaming?
No, John, you are living.
Are you sure?
Up.
Up.
Flat.

In New York.
Warm feet in new socks.
That's me through customs!
Is God this powerful?
Yes, Harold, more powerful than madness.
Are you sure?
Mile. Mile. Mile. Miles.

In life in exile, everywhere:
Love without solution.
That's one of them again!
Surely now he must go into exile?
All reasonable people would.
Love.
Love.
Love.

In exile.
Questions without feeling.
When did you come?
When are you going home, as soon as possible?
Surely your people still need you?
Can we help you with anything?
Bye. Bye. Bye.

In exile.
Curiosity killed a cat. Then me.
Are you happy here?
What about your health?
Do you like our food?
What can we do to help?
Terrible. Terrible. Terrible.

In exile.
Sympathy without limit.
Do your children have clothes?
And your wife?
Do you feel safe here?
Will you go home?
Shame. Shame. Shame.

In exile.
Health for public scrutiny.
What's wrong with you if I may ask?
Anything wrong with you physically and mentally?
Do you go to the hospital every day?
What do they do?
Curiosity. Curiosity. Curiosity.

In exile.
Ignorance and prejudice.
Do you have a house at home?
Do people drink tea and eat rice?
Where did you learn English?
Can you drive a car?
Hmmm! Hmmm! Hmmm!

In exile.
Underestimated, devalued.
This is a pot.
Your lights are here.
Have you ever used a fridge?
You flush here after use.
See. See. See.

In exile.
Appreciated, loved through and through.
Call me at any time for anything.
Are you available for picnic and dinner?
We've done a little, can we do more?
Few of us realize that blacks are adults, not children.
Learning. Learning. Learning.

In exile.
Insulted, hatred.
Undress ma'am. Customs check up.
EEC passports this side. All others that side.
You won't take up a job, will you?
What a comfortable apartment! We ourselves can't even afford this.
Kings. Kings. Kings.

In exile.
Respected, valued.
We can learn much from you.
How is our country in your people's eyes?
Thank you for your sermon. Come again.
We love to visit you. If you have time.
Humanity. Humanity. Humanity.

In exile.
Racism. Globalism. Suspicion.
Come next Sunday.
Stay put my wife is sick.
Come next Friday.
Wait my kid is sick.
Come next month, date will come.
Be patient, wife on duty.
Now, let's make it tomorrow.
Sorry, wife's father taken suddenly ill.
Come tomorrow for ice cream. Sorry for wife's absence.
No, can't postpone it, on wife's return we'll be too busy.
Communists would love to take over your country.
Whites are not that bad are they?
Would blacks ably run the country without whites?
You are fed better than rest of Africa, aren't you?
My grandfather was missionary in Tanzania, says
people eat their kids and cow dung.
You look good these days. Healthy looking.
Your kids at school? European things too tough for them, eh?

In exile.
Love. Hate. Safety. Insecurity. Privacy. Exposure. Question marks!
East, West, home is best.
North, South, home is center.
Safety, Security, home is life.
Where home and heart meet, milk and honey will flow in the desert.

Confessor of Christ Award: Reply

I am the good shepherd,
I am willing to die for the flock.
A hired man owns no sheep;
He sees a wolf and runs away.
The wolf comes hungry and menacing,
Snatches the sheep and scatters them.

Whose words are these?
What race?
What tribe?
What ideology?
What color?
What sex?
What political affiliation?
What age?

It is the Son of God,
The words of Christ to you and me.
Shall I receive an award in the light of these?
Dare I play brave before the crucified?
Dare I?
Dare you?

On our own, no!
In and through Christ, yes!

Too many have died;
Too many are in exile.
Too many are in prison;
Too many are on trial.
Too many out of school;
Too many are without jobs.

Too many are without vote;
Too many heroes unrecognized and unrewarded.
Millions without medals.
Millions win no prizes.
Millions without awards.
   For they have no titles,
     For they have no university degrees.
        For they speak no English,
           Have not been to Oxford and Cambridge.

>   They are not pastors.
>   They are not deans.
>   They are not presidents.
>   They are not bishops.

All they claim is the image of God,
All they claim is the right to be human:
>   A place under the sun,
>   A spot on the earth.
>   An island in the sea,
>   A place at table,
>   A bite three times a day.
>   Clothes to hide their shame,
>   A roof above their heads.
Access to the ballot box—
>   Only avenue to power without violence!

Do you subscribe to freedom?
Upholders of fairness and justice?
Are you vessels of love?
A visit to prison—
A glass of water to the thirsty—
A morsel to the hungry—
Cover to the naked?
Strange?

Strangers are with us—
Neighborhoods full of widows—
Orphans without mom and dad—
Sick that scream and groan—
For love talent buried in you and me.

Good Samaritan received Confessor of Christ Award,
Not victim along Jerusalem-Jericho road.
Here, victim that I am!
Hear, good Samaritans that you are!
Beware Christ is coming.
Take note you saints of Chicago,
An award mistaken for me,
May be a crown meant for you.

What's life without fear?

When you move without warning,
Loud knocks at the dead of night,
What is life without fear?

When today you are as free as the air,
Next day locked in a banning order,
What's life without fear?

When in October you're housed in five star hotels,
Then in November five stars below the sty,
What's life without fear?

When on Friday you fish with a friend,
And Sunday you comfort his police-made widow,
What's life without fear?

When you go in and out,
And go in and out and in,
What's life without fear?

When scoundrels are honored,
And the guilty convict the innocent,
What's life without fear?

When prisons are full of angels,
And the foul stand guard,
What's life without fear?

When the fearless live in the land of fear,
And the fearful roam the land of the fearless,
Only those living in love dare live without fear!

Alone in company

Muima wo ga shaka ndi nnyi?:
No man is an island.
Alone in a crowd.
Three days through the forest,
No trees in sight,
Have eyes but cannot see.

Not as God intended:

Munwe muthihi a u tusi mathuthu:
Two is company three is none.
Individual in a community.
Hundred years in Jo'burg,
In Soweto not a single day,
Neighbors here but far away.

Not as God intended:

Nyavhumbwa wa dagaila wa kanda vho u vhumbaho:
Bite not the hand that feeds you
White dot in continent large and black.
Three hundred years in isolation,
Loved by all, hated all,
Have ears but cannot hear.

Not as God intended:

Tshinanaunga tshi tshi hula tshi u la thoho.
Killing the goose that lays golden eggs.
Political majority, numerical minority.
Drowned in self-inflicted fear,
Every black face a potential friend,
But enemies all around you see.

Not as God intended:

Wa vhona mbulu we mbumbu mudamurahu u de mbulu yanga:
Make hay while the sun shines,
For the hour comes when no man can work.
White to white is a monologue,
Black and white is a dialogue.
Nobody to talk to yet so many around you.

Not as God intended:

Nyadzawela vhanwe wa sea matshelo dzi do u wela-vho:
Laugh not at the handicapped,
Tomorrow you lose your toe.
Many were rich that are poor,
Lords are they who used to serve,
Christ was Lord yet servant of all.

As God intended:

Vhana vha khotsi vha thukhukana thoho ya nzie:
They are God's that are tall.
They are God's that are short.
They are God's in mansions.
They are God's in the ghettos.
They are God's with golden rings.
They are God's who dress in the green of nature.

As God intended:

Beyond the paint is the image of God.
Beneath the surface is the likeness of the king.
Not a baboon in human disguise,
Not an attempt left unfinished,
Not a flaw in His workmanship:
Beneath the paint is Christ in disguise.

What a lonely crowd:

Behind a laager of fear and fraud,
Enslaved by power and stolen privilege,
    A nation for which Christ has died!
Come home prodigals,
Come home to Africa.
One human race black and white,
One human race dumb and talking,
One human race on foot and horseback,
One human race in space and mother earth,
One human race in Asia and Africa,
One human race in America and Europe,
One human race in Australia and Greenland.
One planet one human race.
One God one people.
One image one quality.
Muima wo ga shaka ndi nnyi?
No man is an island.

Rest in peace

This mighty lake,
My newfound mate,
The huge expanse before my face,
That disappears behind the haze.

Behind me she lies in peace.
Back in the room kids lie a piece.
Old memories meander in the back,
Ahead prospects that unfold like a flag.

I shall not gaze into space.
I shall not look into the heavens.
On the blue mass that roll and roar,
Floats my mind that gloat and roam.

In solitude I'm not alone.
Alone I'm not lonely:
Here is my self that hides in the crowd.
Here is God unfettered by men and women of the cloth.

Were I as free as the swallow that swims the air!
Were I as fresh as the fish unmarked by nightmare!
I would dance like the grass on my left.
I would sing like the wind at God's behest.
Like the dead fish on the sand,
Like my new-found peace in this land.

In our own right

From the concrete forest,
To far far away.
Away from lanes,
Away from avenues,
Away from malls,
To far far away.

From humans that greet and wait for no response,
To nature's home far away.
To a house that is home,
To people that are humane,
To food that has taste,
To far far away.

From a cave that's called a house,
To a house that's called a cave.
I love the raccoon that visits by day.
I love the raccoom that feeds by night.
The virgin water in the marsh,
Tall trees that dwarf giant and pygmy.

Free from protocol of procedure and formality of status:
We eat what we want.
We sleep when we want.
Life free from watches,
Conduct unmonitored by watchers,
Freedom that only Adam and Eve could know.

Klein Kaatjies* and Little Kittens

Five wives to every man,
Six kittens to every woman,
One male kitten to every five,
Five kaffirs to every white,
Birth control our only weapon.

White women gather courage.
Multiply and fill the earth,
Boys and girls in equal numbers,
Large families without limit,
Let Canaan decrease while you increase.

One maid to every basie,
Nonnie needs tender care.
Three baths every day,
Four good meals that nourish and heal,
Our kids need tender grass.

Too many kittens in town these days.
Klein kaatjies dirty and weak,
Spreading malnutrition among our own,
Coughing blood without restraint,
Tummies bulging like kaffir drums.

    Immigration will see us through!

---

*Afrikaans word for small kittens.

Existence in transit

Born aborigines,
Grew up natives,
Died kaffirs,
   Always in transit.

Born kaffirs,
Graduated Bantu,
Buried Non-white,
   Always in transit.

Born non-white,
Turned non-European,
Ended up Colored,
   Always in transit.

Born Colored,
Changed to Cape Colored,
Other-colored in epitaph,
   Always in transit.

Born African,
Raised plural,
Sentenced to cooperative,
   Always in transit.

Born South African,
Citizenship unidentified,
Corpse Venda citizen,
   Always in transit.

Born one country,
Divided into eleven,
Eighty-seven percent one, thirteen percent ten,
   Always in transit.

Once had a vote,
Then little voice,
Then nothing,
   Always in transit.

Now born human,
Now raised black,
Ever black shall be,
   Always in transit.

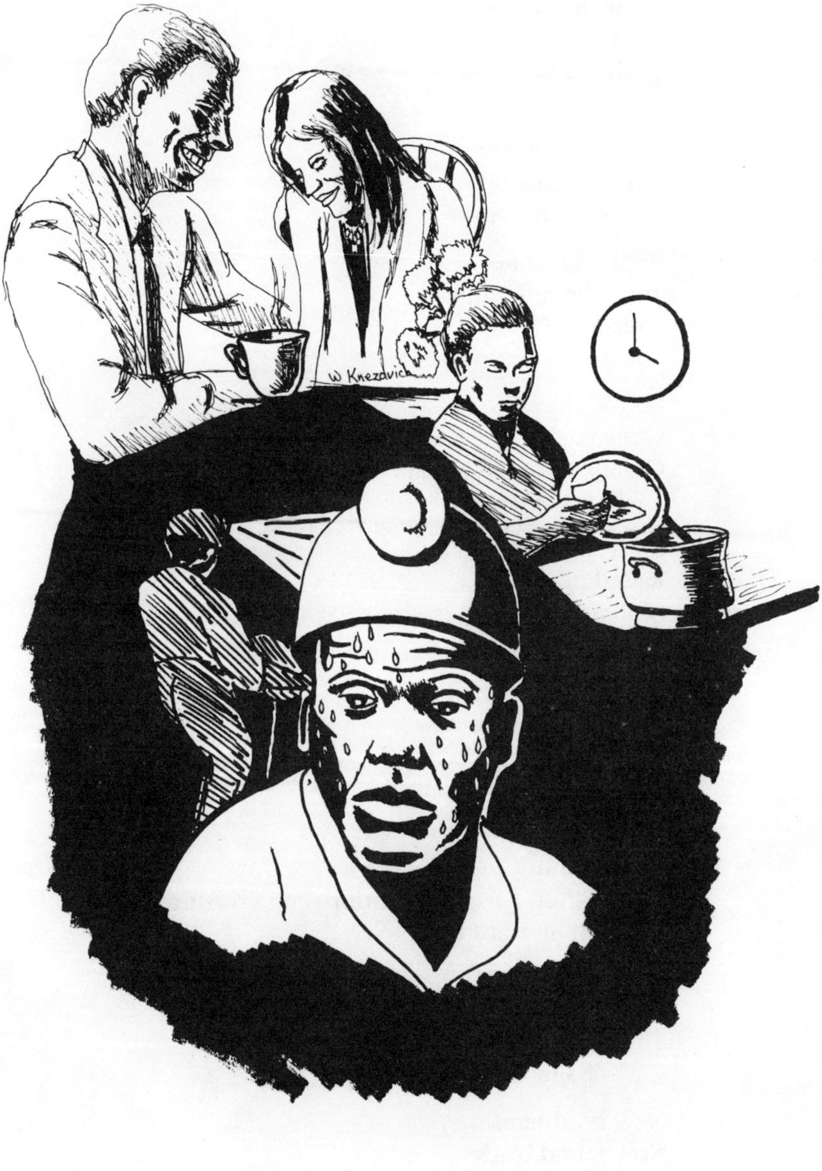
W Knezovich

Do black laborers feel?

Away from home . . . . .
    Tranquil in solitude . . . . .
Polite in his manners . . . . .
    Yet quick to his banners . . . . .
Single sex hostel his home . . . . .
    Married to himself . . . . .
Home base six hundred kilometers away . . . . .
    Even in this cold month of May . . . . .

In the posh suburb of Hillbrow . . . . .
    Up at four o'clock . . . . .
She mixes flour and milk . . . . .
At seven Missis and Baas will be up . . . . .
    Hungry and ready to break their fast . . . . .
Her crippled miner husband back in Transkei . . . . .
    She must fend for kith and kin . . . . .

On the potato farm in fertile lands of Bethal . . . . .
    Every back bent in obedient service . . . . .
On Zebedida estates of orange and mandarin . . . . .
    Every black neck raised giraffe style . . . . .
In the maize triangle laboring ten hours a day . . . . .
    Part-time wages for full-time laborers . . . . .
In the mines that spew gold and diamonds . . . . .
    Trapped in poverty and methane gas . . . . .

At theological college

Before I was sent
To theological college
I was told
That I must be honest
And sincere
In everything I do

My bishop warned me
Against hate
He taught me
How to behave
And how to pray
Every morning and every night

Everything is God's will
Said my rector
He is rector by
God's will
We are students
And also black and oppressed by God's will

My lecturers told me
Not to complain
The lion feeds on the buck
Not on grass by God's will
When whites rule and blacks obey
God has made it so

Fifty rands for black lecturers
Hundreds and thousands for white staff
Whites have many needs
Blacks not so many
Little wages for black laborers
No pension at all

Will gogo the old
Working ten hours a day
Will ntombi the young woman
Working seven days a week
Will Indoda the young man
Not be compensated for their sweat

Houses for whites in the holy land
Dormitories for blacks and coloreds apart
Court for gentiles
Court for women
Court for Israel
Holy of holies in the land of apartheid

There is a church near the college
For blacks, Kamphausen and Lochmann
Other whites to white Hermannsburg
No spirit of cooperation
No spirit of unity
No body of Christ.

Natural pairs

Satan is black...
Black is Satan...
God is white...
White is God...
White is beauty...
Brown is fair...
Black is unplaced.

Hands and feet...
White and riches...
Black and poverty...
White and God...
Black and Satan...
White and paradise...
Black and hell.

Democracy and justice...
White and politics...
Black and agitation...
White and Sem...
Pale and Japhet...
Black and Ham...
Master and slave....

My congregant My Judas Iscariot

By birth human—
  By confession Christian—
    By color black—
      Lutheran in denomination—
      All round my friend—

An elder by standing—
  A liturgist in talent—
    Sang liturgy before my sermon—
      Carried my briefcase with hymn and Bible—
      My congregant all round.

Taken as municipal officer by all around—
  Supported church by funds and prayer—
    Transported angels from house to compound—
      Bought me milk and butter across the border—
      All round my congregant full of love—

On November 18, 1981—
  Leading a gang vicious and vengeful—
    My disciple pointed a finger at me—
      For my soul that melted within me—
      Thirty pieces would come his way—

Lucifer turned into darkness—
  Drove me long distance to the north—
    Dropped me at Masisi the place of skulls—
      Tore my spiritual tracts into shreds—
      My man is in fact their man—

He came on November twenty-third—
  Again on November twenty-fifth—
    Again on January 4, 1982—
      And on the next day—
      Spitting fire all the way—

My swollen head is partly his work—
  My punctured ear drum his handiwork—
    On my knees and elbows are his scars—
      Ears and genitals carry marks of electric shocks—
      When friend turns into foe—

Judas Iscariot I meet now every week—
His face is drawn and eyes are red—
Away from Church and away from God—
Help me pray for this prodigal son—
To make him bask in the grace of the son.

Prisoner outside Prison walls

Tears welled in my eyes,
My manhood disappeared.
From the man behind bars,
They had removed his beard.

I cried like a baby.
I did not look like a daddy.
Man turned into torture machine,
His conscience they had removed.

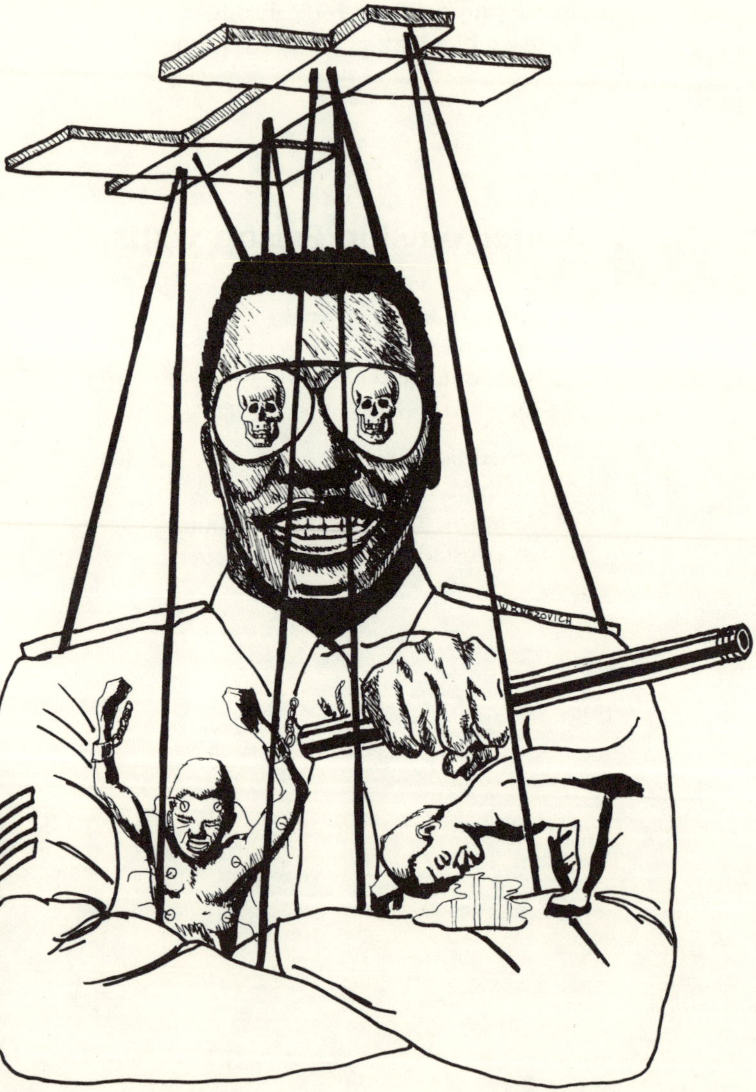

The Beast man

Hairy all the way,
Ligaments tight and taut,
Eyeballs rolling in the cave,
Muscles rolled on thighs and arms,
Tiny head above shoulders broad and square,
Lion man except for two legs.
   Jy sal die waarheid praat—
      You will tell the truth.

Left hook—enemy of my country!
Upper cut—Communist!
Right hook—Terrorist!
Punch below the belt—bloody kaffir!
Combination of lefts and rights—taste white power!
Dinosaur in full blood.
   Jy sal die waarheid praat of jy sal dit uitkak—
      You will tell the truth or you will shit it.

Four days without sleep,
Four days without food,
Four days and four nights without rest,
No response to nature's call.
Psychological torture, violence all the way,
Mauled by white rhinoceros.
   Jy gaan praat of jy gaan vrek—
      Talk you must or you shall die.

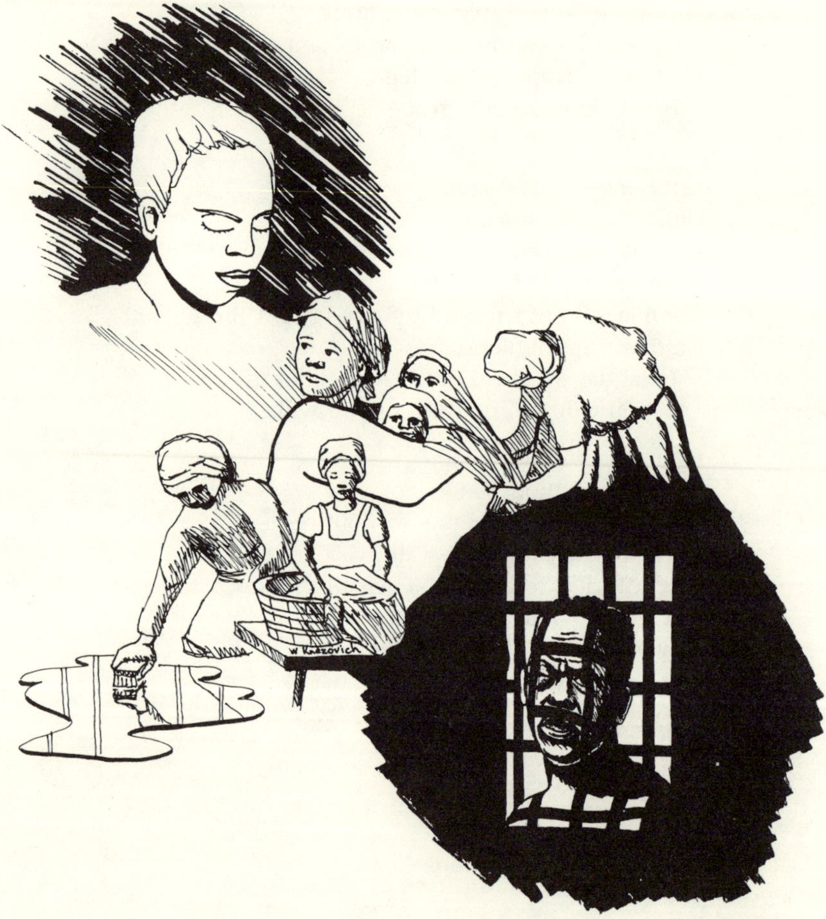

We owe these women

When we are gone,
When we are in,
Locked behind bars,
Alone in the cell,
Alone they run the home.

When we are flat,
When we are down,
Tucked in solitary confinement,
Alone in hell,
Alone they keep our hope.

When we are dirty,
When we are smelly,
Rolling in frustration,
Alone in the hole,
Alone they give us company.

When we are low,
When we've ceased to glow,
Lost in the land of ghosts,
Alone in Masisi,
Alone they send us clothes.

When we are beaten,
When we are wounded,
Lying mauled in hospital,
Alone in deathrow,
Alone they rekindle our fire.

When we are drowning,
When we are defeated,
Licking our wounds on rib and knee,
Alone on the frontline,
Alone they oil our festering wounds.

When we are marched to court on all fours,
When we must sign or forfeit our sigh,
Sandwiched between need and zeal,
Alone in the firing line,
Alone they hold up the hand of a tiring Moses.

When they knock on the door,
When we tremble and crumble from within,
Called to serve suffer and sacrifice,
Alone in the home,
Alone they hold the line.

When we are cornered and crowded,
When we are dumb and dull,
Anesthetized by fear and gloom,
Alone without the crowd,
Alone they clear our minds.

When for days and months we are no more,
When for years and decades we froth and frown,
Gracing Robben Island and Pollsmoor,
Alone in no-man's-land,
Alone they carry the umthwalo* of uhuru.

When we are shouted and shattered,
When we are browbeaten and silenced,
Bundled into the coffin of the living,
Alone in the struggle for the goal,
Alone they keep the posts.

When we shall win and wind our days,
When we shall rule and run our lives,
Sandwiched between power and dream,
All of us picking off the uhuru tree,
Alone they shall deserve the crown.

Verwoerd. Vorster. Botha. Successor,
　"Now you have touched the women,
　You have struck a rock,
　You have dislodged a boulder,
　You will be crushed."
These valiant women:
We owe them much:
Our love. Our life. Our faith. Our everything.

---

*Umthwalo of uhuru: freedom burden.

Think small—talk small—act small

Call God white—
    and he'll be as white as snow.
Call God black—
    And you'll find him in the ghetto.
See God in capitalist glasses—
    And he'll be in Whitehall.
See Satan as communist—
    And he'll operate from Moscow.
What you sow,
That you reap,
What you reap,
That you sow,
What you sow,
That you reap.

Break the vicious circle.

Call man a baboon—
    Next day he is on all fours.
Call her monkey—
    Tomorrow she'll jump from branch to branch.
Call them dogs—
    They'll bark through and through.
Call them subversives—
    Soon you'll find them all under ground.
Call it me,
It I shall be,
I shall be it,
What you call me,
Call it me,
It I shall be.

You are aborigine—
    And so I am.
You are native—
    And so I am.
You are kaffir—
    And so I am.
You are bantu—
    And so I am.

A non-white tag—
 Non-South African alien.
A non-European label—
 Non-being badge.
A non-resident pass—
 A non-worker permit.
A non-person labor force—
 Persona non grata.

Amnesty International

We may not know the person.
We may not know the number.
We may not know the camp.
We may not know the conditions.
    We do not know the date.
    We do not know the place.
    We do not know the police.
    We do not know the methods.
All we know all will know:
    People are born free.
    Innocent shall remain free.
    Justice to all colors,
    Fairness to all cultures,
    Equality to male and female,
    Jewish by faith free,
    Islam by faith free,
    Christian by faith free,
    Capital punishment to none,
    Torture to all taboo,
    Amnesty International.

We know not the writers,
Group members hidden far beyond.
We know not the cities,
Race far beyond the pale.
    We do not know the sex.
    We do not know the age.
    We do not know the profession.
    We do not know the motive.
All we know all prisoners of conscience will know:
    Amnesty International is neither east nor west,
    A.I. is neither black nor white,
    A.I. is neither male nor female,
    A.I. is neither rich nor poor,
    A.I. is neither game nor fun,
    A.I. is neither neutral nor partisan,
    A.I. is neither Nato nor Warsaw,
    A.I. is neither here nor there,
    A.I. is neither high nor low,
    Amnesty International for you and for me.

In Washington prison A.I. fought for me,
In John Vorster Square A.I. stood by me,
In ice-cold Siberia A.I. spoke for me,
In deathrow A.I. defended my life,
In torture chambers A.I. pleaded for me,
In isolation A.I. became my companion.
When I disappeared A.I. appeared for me,
Found guilty without trial,
A.I. tried the verdict.
Tried without charges,
A.I. charged the court.
Murdered in the name of law,
A.I. fouled the law.
Was once forgotten,
Now I'm known.
Sentenced to life,
Now I live.
Disgraced for justice,
Now I'm honored.
Trodden down,
Now I'm up.
In barbed wire,
Flickers a flame of hope,
The candle burns on,
The oil of freedom,
In a world gone mad,
Burns the flame of sanity.

Called devil by Satan,
Called Satan by the devil,
Yet neither evil nor crooked.

Called west by east,
Called east by west,
By the north despised,
By the south maligned,
Yet neither south nor north,
Neither east nor west,
Amnesty International all around.

Killer permits

Our ancestors died free.
Ten generations back we were kings and masters of our own destiny.
Greatgrandfather was part of it.
Makhulukuku saw part of it.
   Now we are slaves by permits—
   Now we are people by permits—
   Now we work by permits—
   Now we eat by permits—
   No permission to be.

Makana and Tshaka died free.
Eight generations back were kings in full degree.
Sekhukhuni was part of our freedom.
Makhulu saw parts of it.
   Now life by pass—
   Now life by act—
   Now life by statute—
   Now life by decree—
   No room to be.

Old years and old moons passed and died free,
Six generations back were men and women in full measure.
Makhado was part of our humanity.
Mmemuhulu saw part of it.
   No work by permit—
   No visit by permit—
   No site by permit—
   No person by permit—
   Enough room to be.

Disease and war killed free men and women,
Four generations back lived blacks threatened but free.
King Moshweshwe was part of our self-determination.
King Sobhuza saw part of it.
   Now we cough by permit—
   Now we piss by permit—
   Now we are colored by permit—
   Now we are urban by permit—
   No right to be.

  When the missionary coveted and "converted" us we were a strong and
     proud people,

Two generations back our faith was fact and firm.
Masekela was part of our dream,
My mother saw part of it.
   Now we worship by race—
   Now we congregate by group areas—
   Now for exegesis we use ideology—
   Now God is our tribe—
   No place to be image of God.

In Sharpeville they mowed down men and women of Africa.
In our generation they face the moment of truth.
Steve Biko was part of the great truth,
Isaac Muofhe saw part of it.
   Cut back the tree it shall grow again—
   Moon will wane but shine again—
   This winter Vhembe is dry, next summer in flood—
   Today white is king, tomorrow without a crown.
   Of virtue victory's born, of vice fall and shame.

In 1976 protests floods by masters of fear,
June 16 bullets by slaves of fear.
Hector Peterson was part of the struggle;
At a distance I saw part of it.
   Now all deaths born of police bullets—
   Now no funeral without permit—
   Four hundred mourning tears within the law—
   Four hundred and one crimes of treason—
   You shall mourn from nine to twelve—
   One after twelve sing songs of Zion—
   Songs of joy in apartheid land—
   Songs of joy by widow and orphan—
   Songs of freedom by slave and serf—
   Songs of life by dead and dying—
   All in honor of god at death—
   Apart from man and away from God—
   Apartheid killer permit.

Moving into the net

I must be mad
To go this way
Back to apartheid land
Where blows land

I must be back
Back in my land
Where people matter
In the land of no butter

Backed by the hand of God
Hounded by aparthate dogs
Wounded by hogs in the fog
Back into the water as a frog

I must be sane
In the land of the profane
To venture this way
When others go the other way

Shall I regret the day
When I had my day
Far far away
Unfettered by the net
Moving into the net
Till Uhuru day.

Little big ones

Act, act, act Superman
  Actor man!
    Actor husband!
      Actor father!
        Actor soul!
          Actor governor!
            Actor president!
              Actor Republican!

Move, move, move Iron lady
  Immovable woman!
    Immovable wife!
      Immovable mother!
        Immovable spirit!
          Immovable commoner!
            Immovable Prime Minister!
        Granite Briton!

Change, change, change Herrenvolk
  Inedible cabbage!
    Inedible salad!
      Inedible vegetable!
        Inedible vitamin!
          Inedible policies!
            Inappropriate chancellor!
        Racist Caucasoid!

Mother love

Your person—
   short and tough
   ready and prepared
   for days and ways ahead
True to your form—
   thorough of thought
   thorough bred
   royal blood in your veins.

Your courage—
   as you work in the fields
   removing the weeds between the seeds
   to feed strangers and kith and kin.
Tuned to your nature—
   fierce and fiery in the sun
   calm and tranquil in the cold
   freedom streams in your bones.

Your firm stand—
   As you discipline a son and daughters five
   Facing dad in his boots
   Confounding me with my books
Towed by hands of time—
   Stood your ground among women
   Firmed lips before the gods
   Changed faith in the face of all.

Your durability—
   assailed by disease of ill degree
   pushed and pulled from side to side
   dragged and drubbed by man and nature.
Tunneled by trial and temptation—
   You emerged strong with scars of sorrow
   Valleys of sleepless nights cut on your face
   Facing the unknown unfold without gold.

Your sacrifice—
   as four times I was dragged before your face
   four times as sonless as you came
   four times your life in exchange
   for only son in grip of death.

Tied to your words—
    Run me over to cover my tears
    Push me down to drown my sorrows
    Let me die and not my son
    Kill me first before my son.

Your prayer life—
    All songs on your twisted lips
    Commandments at your beck and call
    Moving library of bible stories
    dwarfing the tallest among professors.

Tailing Christ all the way—
    Mocked for Christ and beaten for Jesus
    Undressed for faith and starved for the cross
    Persecuted by fate and institution
    Crawling on and on the via dolorosa.

Your love for the neighbor—
    No woman of the cloth
    You clothed the naked
    No woman of letters
    You counseled professors.

Your willingness to share—
    Sharing something when you had none
    Giving all when you had some
    A better pastor I've not met
    You shame the rich and enrich the poor.

Your patience robust and round—
    As we all leave you alone and old
    As your only son you see no more
    daughter-in-law and grandchildren three
    Detained by distance beyond the pale.

Hold on mom to hope and cope—
    If you die alone and broke
    As we linger along foreign coasts
    Know one thing I've not told
    Your will-of-love, longer than life
    We'll pass on to generations unborn
    Hope we've loved you too.

Man beast

Also in the image of God
Also in the mould of man
   Rounded capital above his shoulders
   Two round eyes like a ball
   Two ears wide like an antennae
   Nostrils as wide as a tunnel
   Not on fours like you and me

His father and mother are like yours and mine
His home is in the homeland dust at the government's whim
   His human pictures hang on the walls
   His human smiles charm his kids
   To Maria a husband all round
   To his parents a son indeed
   Not on four like you and me

Every dawn to dusk at work like you and me
Every square inch black and bantu unintended
   Above the capital black hair thick and curly
   Above thick lips broad nose flat and muscular
   Only enough white paint for his teeth
   Only enough white for palms and soles
   Not on fours like you and me

At work he undresses the human gown
On duty a baboon in human guise
   Joining hands with hands not his own
   He throws his anger against his own
   Blessing his master and cursing his fellow-slave
   He carves his future on a rock of butter
   Not on fours like you and me

When at day's end his work is done and his victims undone
He dons his gown and treads the human path
   He shakes every hand along the way
   He takes off his hat to young and old
   Only his wife will smell tonight
   Guilty blood flowing down his veins
   Not on fours like you and me

I met him at Howick the other day
Among the snowies lost to his own

In his masters' choir he sang their songs
As his masters' voice he spoke their language
When they kicked he kicked with them
When they stopped he failed to stop
Not on fours like you and me

Our paths crossed at Louis Trichardt prison
Both of same stock divided by a wall of greed
    To me he spat venom to his mentor's glee
    Cutting his nose to spite his face
    He strutted like a cock but could not crow
    In two weeks he won a sergeant's badge
    Not on fours like you and me

At Masisi I met both man and beast in one
Vacillating between man and dinosaur
    In a white suit he could have been Michael the angel
    In his fury the king of hell
    Soft water down granite cataracts
    A dove in a boxer's ring
    Not on fours like you and me

At Cana water changed into wine
At Sibasa man became beast
    He opened his mouth to speak but roared
    He touched buttons for light and produced shock
    At his Christian music Satan leapt in a dance
    At his hallelujah the Lord fell into a trance
    Not on four like you and me

The Lord is the same yesterday, today and forever
In their hands we're moulded into anything like clay
    Dear doctor dear man of God
    May God bless you amen
    Dear son of a witchdoctor
    Hypocrite and professional liar fit for torture
    Not on all fours like you and me

It is not a choice between east and west

Like father
Like son
In father's will
Is the son's lot
Here lies my heritage:
In his image all my life
Like him all my days
His image my only pass.

Like father
Like son
In father's cabinet
Is the son's post
Here is my share:
In his cabinet all my days
Controlling world and all in it in father's fashion
His image my only pass.

Father loves me dearly
I like my father too
In his world there's movement for me
At his table my daily bread
Here is my dividend:
Sunrise and rainfall without color
Breath and digestion without fee
His image my only pass.

Father like me
I love him too
I was black and his son died for me
An outcast I hosted his son
Here's my worth before his eye:
Hungry he fed me
Thirsty he gave me drink
Stranger he took me in
Naked he clothed me
Prisoner he visited me
His image my only pass.

We choose not between east and west
Our vote not for north or south

Whoever stands for my right to be
Whoever visits me in apartheid ghetto
Is willing to veto apartheid life
Is willing to dump bloodied gold
Walks hand in hand with my dream
Denies not my own refuge
Denounces evil beyond word and posture
And feeds not his own in my name
His party wins my only vote
Whose hand stretches forth
To pick my brother in the dust
Between Jerusalem and Jericho
Between Messina and Cape Town.

Tit for tat and butter for fat

A person who
brutalizes another
will become an animal.

A man who
hates
will be hated.

Whoever
kills
will die of the sword.

A woman
who mocks
will be ridiculed.

A race
that crushes another
will be razed to the ground.

Whoever
sows the seeds of fear
will himself flee from a fly.

They cannot sleep
for they know
that we are not asleep.

Are you an honorary God O Lord?

You gambled and lost O God:
You gave a finger and lost a hand.
You gave us your image:
Now lost in the damage of race.
Whites are human no more.
Blacks have lost their core.
Yellow and brown our only bore,
Colored born of an honorary god,
Japanese born of an honorary god,
Chinese born of an honorary god,
Indians born of an honorary God,
When the apartheid god speaks:
Gold, all offer their fingers;
Coal, all do the deal;
Uranium, human rights to hell;
Chrome, black freedom can wait;
Platinum, more precious than life;
Business, up the whites and down the niggers.

You gambled on multicolored humanity O God:
You shared power and lost control.
We dumped our gods to adopt an image,
Went on our knees as they stole our land.
We fed on manna and relish of quail,
As they pillaged our gold and plundered our land.
Now glued to the Bible and Sinai desert,
Eking a living on body and blood shed for us,
Fasting our way to heaven through the land of plenty,
Washing white laundry and worshiping their god.
As Verwoerd marches in the footsteps of Moses,
And like Joshua John Vorster forges ahead,
While Botha comes to divide and rule:
Shem to the right and Ham to the left,
Japhet on top and Canaan below,
Here begins paradise for new Israel,
Now begins hell for Ham the bantu,
Till the second coming of Hitler and Verwoerd.

Will evil people gamble on your name O God?
On your son's garmet they gambled and lost.

On Bentura Visser bold men won all battles but lost the war.
Anna Steenkamp lost reason but won the racist trek.
Apartheid lost pronounced while winning active support.
A god of love lost to a god of hate,
A god of all lost to a god of some,
A real god to an honorary god.
We worshipped up and lost the earth below,
When we faced down we retained our land.
Until you rise we shall know for sure, you
An honorary god with us in the slum,
Like your son who picked us from the mud.

Too clean

When angry
They curse.
When wronged
They are angry.
They are human
Have flesh and blood.
Something's wrong with me
Mr. Too Clean.
Ineffective.

When the Boers were angry
They cursed the British.
When they were wronged
They fought back.
That's human.
Something's wrong with me
Mr. Non-Violent.
Unproductive.

Hitler felt robbed,
And fought.
Britain felt challenged,
And fought.
When the United States feels challenged,
They attack.
What's wrong with me Mr. Pacifist?
My faith.

Thank God I am free

As I look
back across
I can only see
Evil man's design
To crush my soul
And crash my life
Against the wall
Of history and time
And yet I'm free

As I walk
in the street of life
I can only hear
Unkindly shouts
To insult my person
And drown my image
Into the ocean
Of race and fate
And yet I'm afloat

As I work
In labor camps
I can only feel
Piercing looks
Uprooting my being
Flouting my worth
At ten cents a day
Down down the drain
Feeding greed and groan
And yet I live

As I bend
In Tshikota township
I can only smell
Bucketfuls of shit
Assaulting my nose
Blunting my appetite
Frustrating my meal
At the poor man's table
And yet I'm as fragrant as the tulip

As I sit
On a garbage bin
I can only taste
My salty tears
Flowing on every cheek
Whetting my anger
Against my oppressor
Feasting on tenderloin
And yet I swallow
      swallow
           swallow
               mellow.

Can't be so bad

They sing a song of joy as they go to work;
They ululate as they weed the farms acre by acre.
How can they be so unhappy?
   How on earth oppressed?
      Denied birthright?
         In the land of their birth?
           Who's so bad?
              Not we
              Whites
              Untrue.

Staffriders jump on and off the moving train,
To the cheers of many they fall and die in song,
How can they be unsatisfied with life?
   How's their freedom of movement denied?
      Forbidden to dangle on death branch?
         In their land of Soweto?
           Who's so autocratic?
              Not we
                 Christians
                 False.

Down the shaft they sing unzima lomthwalo;
Five miles underground they sing the burden is easy.
How can they be underpaid?
   They touch gold every day and every night.

      Blinding diamonds shine into their dark brown eyes,
        As they smash rock and granite apart,
          As far as they can go.
            We whites on the black man's way?
              Not we
              Civilized
              Wrong.

God is a government in his own right.
Who voted him into office?
All governments are from above.
    How can ours be so bad?
        Never have so few done so much for so many:
            Barbarians turned to people,
            Voters in their homelands.
                Aren't we benefactors
                  Doing right?

Basotho flock across borders in full delight.
Amaswati thank their gods for a place in our sun.
    How can ours be devil's own land?
        Why feed at Satan's table?
            Even though the spoon be long?
                Where would they be without us?
                  Al drap 'n aap 'n goue ring,
                      Hy bhy maar nog in lelike ding.*

---

*Although an ape wears a golden ring he remains an ugly thing.

Sin once and for all in one spurt of rage

Bloody white pigs who robbed us of our land and raped our country women and resources and stole everything precious to us including our humanity ugly devils with long noses and cruel behavior who hobnob with Satan in their thefts of our lives and our rightful possessions let us throw them and their ugly fat kids into the ocean and feed the sharks that are starving like us shoot their women on their thin buttocks and shoot their daughters and sons who feed on our blood kill all whites until none is left of this cursed race that was thrown down from heaven damned Lucifer thrown into our country to kill and oppress let us put away our love and our patience and destroy them all young and old taking away our houses and cars and cities and farms and roads and factories and government which they have stolen let us do it fast before God comes back from his vacation on the island of negligence I see him coming before I sin thank you God I nearly ran mad to kill them all do I have a sin to confess for planning my freedom sorry for plan not for freedom.

I feel like giving in

When I look at the odds:
The mountain to climb,
The valley to cross,
The price to pay,
I feel like giving in.

When I study my opposition:
Their military gear,
The rippling muscles,
Their bloodied hands,
I feel like giving in.

When I visit the graveyard:
I see Shezi's grave,
Tshikhudo's unmarked grave,
And a space for my own,
I feel like giving in.

When I turn to my marked body:
And see scars on the wrists,
Marks on the kneecaps,
And another in-between,
I feel like giving in.

But for the ghost of Shakespeare:
"Cowards die many times before their death,
the valiant never taste of death but once."

Living for my children I must die for them

Nzumbu deserves a father;
She is a beautiful girl.
But unless I fight
And die for her,
She will never taste
What it is like
To be a woman.

Ndamu needs a father;
She's cute.
But unless I risk
My life and all,
She will never know
What it is like
To walk hand in hand with freedom.

Zwo is like me;
He's a tough boy.
But unless I sacrifice
To serve God and my people,
Will he ever know
Whom to imitate
To be truly a man?

What am I fighting for?

What am I fighting for?
   To throw whitey into the sea?
   To steal their stolen mansions?
   To rape their women?
   And kill their overfed kids?
                    No, I am not.

What are we fighting for?
   To be white or honorary white?
   To do as they've done?
   To starve them and accuse them of a hunger strike?
   To deny them education and blame them for illiteracy?
                    No, we are not.

What have they died for?
   For mentors beyond the imaginary curtain?
   For personal selfish ends?
   For a place among the saints?
   A statue in Heroes Acre?
                    Not fallen freedom fighters.

Why should we not die:
   For porridge to feed our kids?
   For cotton to warm our old?
   For space to put our shelter?
   A paper to make our cross?
                    We voteless citizens of South Africa.

Keep your medicines

I wanted to sit,
Was told to lie down.
When shall I learn to
   SIT?

I tried to walk,
Was told to crawl.
When shall I learn to
   WALK?

I wanted to run,
Was told to walk.
When shall I learn to
   RUN?

I wanted education,
Was given Bantu education.
When shall I receive unlabelled
   EDUCATION?

I wanted to fly,
Was told to plough.
When shall I learn to plough in the
   AIR?

I wanted to fight back,
Was told not to use sanctions.
When shall I learn to use a knock out
   PUNCH?

At a road block

Drums
Drums zebra painted
Drums zebra painted zig-zag lined
Drums zebra painted chained pole to pole
Stop   Halt   Stop

Torches
Torches blue eyed
Torches blue eyed wincing blue blue
Torches blue eyed in the hands of red eye police
Stop   Halt   Stop

Open
Open the trunk
Open the trunk and the hood
Open the door get out open your cases
Mouth   Legs   Arm-pits

Who is this
Who is this and this and that
Whom are you visiting in this place
Whose Bibles and hymns are these
Hmm   Eh   Hmmm

Go on Baas
You stop or I shoot your swartgat*

---

*Afrikaans for "black arse"

Moon

Quarter smile
Love
of
nature
Half smile
Love
of
man
Full smile
Love
of
God
Ocean Tides
High
and
Low
Lift our moods
Up
and
Down
So is power
it
waxes
and
wanes
Blessed are they whose smile is full

The Sun

I went to the bank to get a sum
I went to the shop to get a suit
I left crying for my funds were low
I left naked as paupers do
To bask in the sun free for all

I went by night and lost my way
I walked in the fog and hurt my toe
I needed a flashlight but none was there for free
I needed boots but there was no size for beggars
I waited for the light that guides me free

I went into a tavern to escape the cold
I took a seat and called for beer
I found myself outside in the snow
I need half a crown to warm my body and throat
I wish I were a swallow to emigrate with the sun

I committed a crime and cried to the judge
I hated a man and wished him dead
I pleaded for mercy and got six years
I withdrew my hate and got double back
I called to One whose sun never sets.

Rain

Without you
Where would rivers be?
Without rivers
Where would oceans be?
Without oceans
Where would you be?

Without you
Where would farmers be?
Without you
Where would lakes be?
Without farmers
Who would appreciate you?

Without you
What would be moisture?
Without moisture
What would be rain?
Without water
What form would be rain?

Without you
Who am I?
Without me
What are you?
Air. Liquid. Solid.
Solid. Liquid. Air.

Greed

If there will be a third world war,
A war that will be won by losers
Losers winning everything but their life, it's
Life of greed.

If East and West shall never agree,
And negotiations drag on and on
While wars drain their coffers, it's
Life of greed.

If the North shall grow richer and richer,
And the South poorer and poorer, it's
Life of greed.

If millionaires conceive billionaires,
And beggars crowd the earth with paupers, it's
Life of greed.

If Christians build cathedrals for pianos huge and large,
And fellow believers can't buy a Bible, it's
Life of greed.

If two people occupy a six room house,
While four spend a winter night in the street below,
Christ must surely die again!
To enliven consciences buried in greed.

Created in the image of evil desire

Some think he is hated by all
Some think he is a laughing stock
Some think he is handicapped upstairs
Some think he is an innocent soul
Some think he is an ignoramus
Pretoria believes them all
No wonder they picked him
To pick the apartheid fruit
Earning poverty for all his people
Earning their hatred and anger
To deserve an iron vest
And life behind the fence
Sharing fear with strangers
Whose crimes he now shares
For selling his people's rights
For three pieces of barren land
Fertile only at stomach button
Womb long removed by limpopo strip
Sperms banked along Levubu belt
Now he's king without crown
I do not think so
Here we have a soul
Here we have a creature
Here we have a prisoner
Created in the image of evil desire
To pick apartheid fruit for life and die.

Legal Circus

"Our" government—
"Our" laws—
"Our" executive branch—
"Our" legislative branch—
"Our" judiciary—
Is all white
Is all circus
Legal circus.

In a white court
Prosecuted by white folk
Before white judge
Using white laws
To defend white interests
In a white world
Full of Herrenvolk
Legal circus.

In a black world
In garments of rightlessness
Where people are guilty at birth
Burdened with Adam's and Ham's sins
And crushed with their own
We plead guilty before the white judge
For our blackness but we were not alone
God was also there.

128

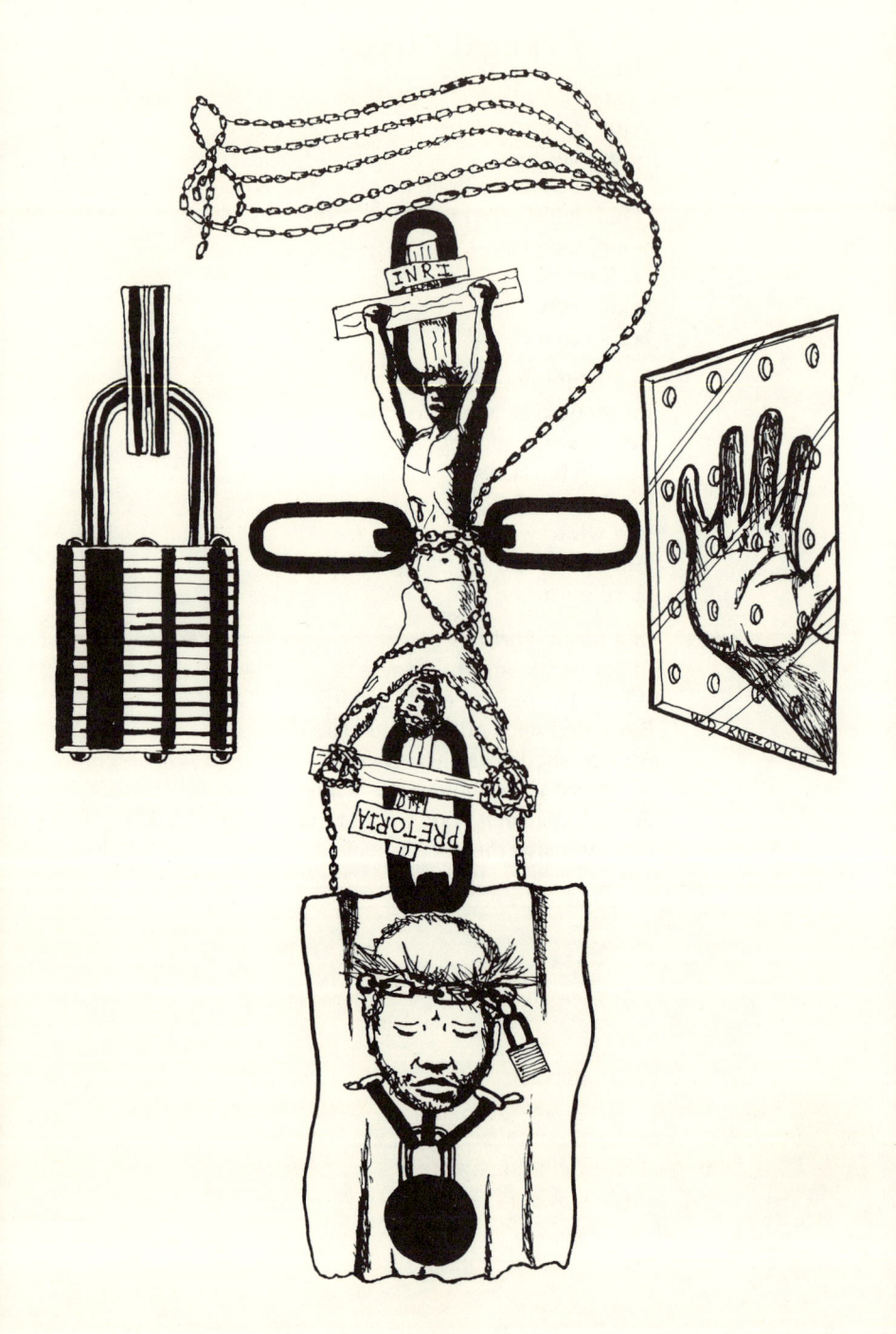

Singing Chains:
A visit to detained Pastor Molefe Tsele

Who is this in chains?
Surely not Pastor Tsele!
Legs in irons?
Chained to another detainee?
In handcuffs?
Tied to another prisoner?
Who is this in chains?

Who is this in chains?
Surely not Molefe, the man of God!
Looks taller than usual?
Hair worn longer and unkept?
In grey sweat pants and faded red sweat shirt?
Warm clothes for cold cells?
Who is this in chains?

Who is this in chains?
God's prophet in John Vorster Square!
Jeremiah in South African Police Headquarters?
Will the passing angel have a glimpse of him?
Before or after Modiehi his wife's visit?
Will his daughter and son see their father?
Who is this in chains?

Who is this in chains?
A Lutheran priest in Dutch Reformed chains!
Husband and wife separated by glass?
Talking through a circle of holes in the glass?
No physical contact between one flesh?
Guard listening to every word and every phrase?
Who is this in chains?

Who is this in chains?
In Pilate's hands accused of saying "thus says the Lord!"
Will Modiehi visit him only for thirty minutes?
Will she leave the door open for my glimpse?
Is this couple consecrated in the name of chains?
Is Adam married to Adam in Eve's eyes?
Who is this in chains?

Who is this in chains?
Christ's disciple upside-down on Pretoria's cross!
Is he smiling at me with his kids in my arms?
Did I smile back or signal some love?
Did I say a word or did he?
Did he flash a thumbs-up at hip-high?
Who is this in chains?

Who is this in chains?
A seer in chains for showing the way to the blind!
Is he a human being like you and me?
Does he love like you and me?
Are his kids like yours and mine?
Does his wife long for his embrace?
Who is this in chains?

What music is that from these chains?
Will man sing in his pain!
Do I hear a freedom song in his heart?
Do I hear amandla from his tight lips?
Freedom streams down his veins?
Victory is certain sing clanging chains?
Who is this with him in chains?

    Is
    it
    the
    Son
    of
    M
    A
    N
    ?

My sword

Without the word
The world would still be chaos.

Without the word
Israel would still be in Egypt.

Without the word
We would still be in sin.

You show me the sword
That's sharper.

You show me the gun
That shoots better.

You show me a bomb
That's more effective.

You show me a more effective punch
That converts Saul without a bloody nose.

You show me a better way
That defeats an enemy into a friend:

The Son of God is my sword;
The word sharper than a two-edged sword.

Change me now

Unless
Changed
Whitefulness
  to
Blacklessness
Unless
Remolded
Greed
  to
Sharing
Unless
Reshaped
Proud
  to
Humble
Unless
Pushed
Suicide
  to
Life
Unless
Converted
Colormaniac
  to
Human
I am
Doomed.

Not in your image

I do not look like you
As I do not eat like you
And talk your language
And walk your style
And love your manners
And play your games
For you did not make me
In your image.

I shall not run my government like yours
As I have watched you
Ruling over me
And other countries like mine
Always putting your interests
Before others' interests
Democracy means I can have my choice
For I am not made in your image.

I do not smile as you do
At a passing fly
And frown at other people
Just because
Their color is unlike mine
I remind you again
That I am not made
In the image of an image.

Sands that break and stick

One rock
Broken into grains
With one identity
Yet sticking together
In a sand dune
Like the original rock
That parts to meet
And meets to part
As all of us in
Adam were one
Mothered by Eve
Mother of all
Now we are grains
Scattered on the shore
And maize grains
Like millet and sorghum
Independent but one race
From human seed
On one stork
With ten cobs
To feed Africa and
Nourish America and
Nurse Asia and
Suck Australia and
Bring up Europe as well
As Greenland.

Now I am ready to die

When
I was a child
I was afraid to die
For the elders told us that to die
Without leaving footprints on a woman's
Womb....

When
I was a boy
I was afraid to kiss
For the grey-haired warned us that to play
Too close to mature girls with deep pools
Drowning.... would result!

Now
I am a man
I am no longer afraid to die
For I have left footprints and swum
The deepest of oceans and still
I am afloat....

Tomorrow
If slow motion bells ring
And you see a widow in black dress
And three children without a father
And with no motion grinning in silence to the sky
Know I'm gone.

Freedom of speech

Presidents
    Prime Ministers
        Premiers
Are slaves of their protocol
Mouthpieces of their parties
Cannot say what they want
In poetry I say what I like!

Kings
    Emperors
        Queens
Are fenced behind tradition
Servants of their crowns
Cannot dress as they want
In poetry I say what I like!

Popes
    Archbishops
        Bishops
Are enslaved in their gowns
Serfs in service of liturgies
Cannot respond to the call of life
In poetry clergy are human,
    National leaders have flesh and blood,
    All have freedom of speech
    To speak through the taboo.

From A to D

First Sunday
  I
Preached and became a
  Jail angel
Second Sunday
  I
Exhorted and became a
  Jail bird
Third Sunday
  I
Reprimanded and became a
  Jail cat
Fourth Sunday
  I
Prophesied and became a
  Jail corpse
Now that
  I
Am silenced and comfortable in a
  Casket
Shall I be
  Silent
The living have life to lose
  Ghosts
Have reason to be feared
  I am still around.

Have you ever

Seen:
the hippo coming down on children?
the caspir rushing through the crowd?
teargas thrown into parsonages?
tearsmoke crashed into churches?
   In Hillbrow?
   In Waterkloof?
   On whites?
     Not as much as in Soweto!

Heard:
a mother called a girl?
a grandfather called a boy?
discrimination called separate and equal?
a man called a baboon?
   On the moon?
   In heaven?
   In hell?
     Not as much as in South Africa!

Witnessed:
a man suspended from a third storey window?
a woman suspended on a stick between two tables?
two bare feet on blunt nails?
Satan condemning an angel?
   Somewhere at the bottom of the sea?
   Somewhere on the planet Mars?
   Or anywhere in between?
     As in Howick!

Heard:
girlish screams from a waarheidkamer?*
a pastor's cry born of electric shock?
powerful music from behind the walls?
amandla shouts from within the dock?
   Four centuries before Christ?
   During the inquisition?
   In the Fuhrer's day?
     As in civilized land!

Believed:
that white is good and gold?

that hard work means good pay?
that for all the sky is the limit?
that black is good as His image?
   In all five continents?
     In every country small and great?
    Everywhere on this planet?
       Unlike our local weather!

---

*truth room (i.e., torture room)

Now's your turn

I
have lived and grumbled
I
have played and worked
I
have cried and laughed
I
have loved and hated
I
have spoken and listened
I
have brought peace and conflict
I
have praised and condemned
I
have been powerless and powerful
  Now
  it
  is
  your
  turn
to know me as I am
to tell me I am too old
to accept my retirement baggage
And watch from the sidelines
As others do it the new way.

We are beaten if those we uphold lose

There was light;
There was night;
God had won—
He upholds them both.

There was oppression;
There was death;
Nobody had won—
It destroys us both.

There was hate;
There was bait;
All were hooked—
We roll now in a frying pan.

There was greed;
There was hunger;
Disease beat both of them—
Now at each other's throat.

There was a will;
There was hope;
None loved to die—
We all are winners.

Hand-to-hand-across-the-land-across-the-planet.

If we

If we go down,
              we go with you.
           we keep you there.
If we go up,
If we go down with disease,
                  we smear you all.
                          that will heighten yours too.
If our life expectancy is high,
If we sweat and earn,
              your losses go down.
                we shall steal and be clean.
If we plant and others harvest,
If we are gunned down,
                it's tools down and guns up.
              the firmament will be permanent.
If we are propped up,
If we are not human,
              all beasts will join us.
If we are both parcel bombs, we better not explode.

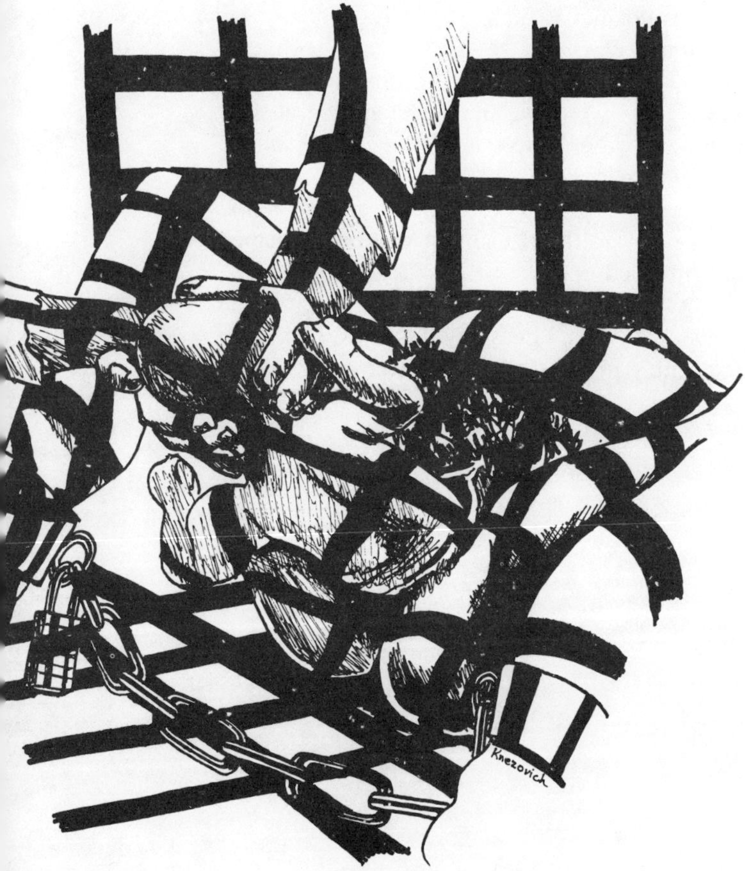
Knezovich

Not meant for each other

Small,
    4 × 4,
Children are not for prisons;
Prisons are not for children.

Bulging,
    4.8 kilogram baby,
Police cell is no maternity ward;
Midwives wear no caps.

Files,
    In a pile,
Medical records are for doctors;
Case numbers for sergeants.

Innocent,
    Free,
Handcuffs are for criminals;
Democrats for medals.

Apartheid,
    Crime,
Apartheid is for the sewage;
Freedom up stream.

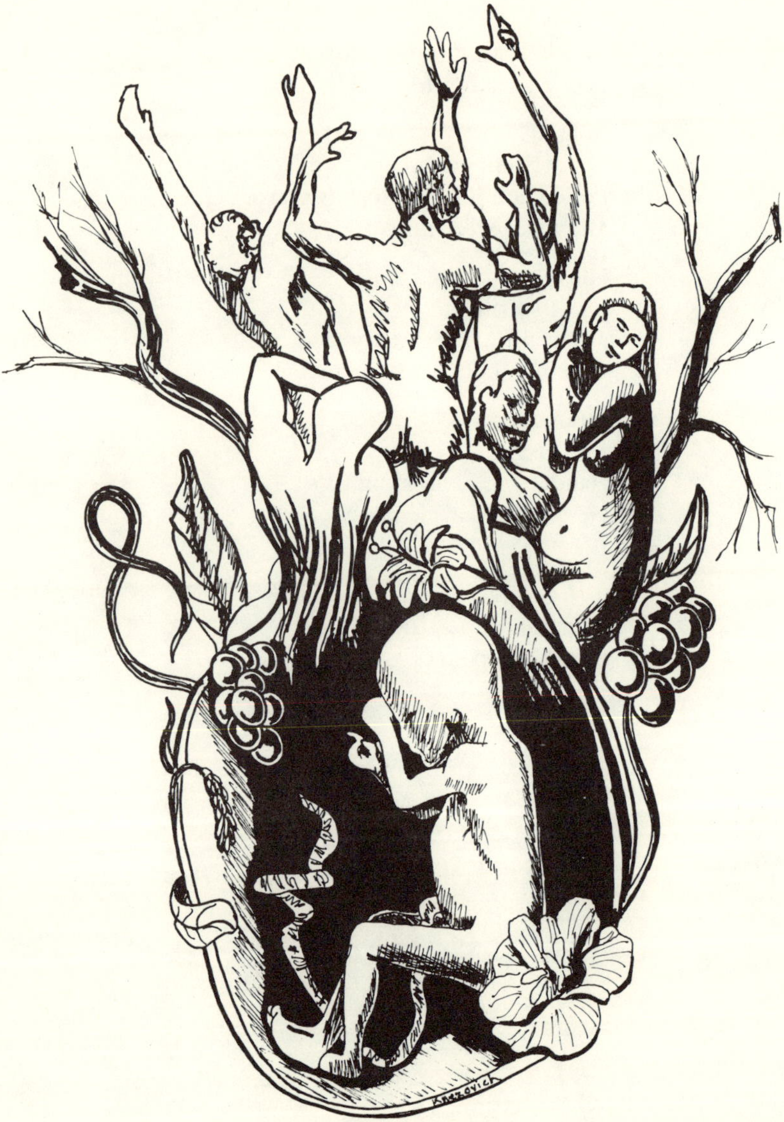

A multiracial tree

A brown stem,
Yellow bark,
Green leaves,
White flowers,
Black fruit,
And yet one tree.

Roots have a culture,
Leaves have customs,
Flowers have beauty,
Leaves chlorophyll,
The stem has posture,
That all is a tree.

Eyes are for sight,
Ears hear,
The nose smells,
Legs walk,
Hands handle,
These all I have.

Are blacks people?
Are browns people?
Are whites people?
Are yellows people?
Are women and men people?
A wonderful human race—a multiracial tree.

Home

Home, bereaved home! Where tears flow
Daughter buried in her palm,
For brother on the run:
Away from piercing torches and a knock on the door,
From owls that feed on human flesh,
To hide his little life in his little palm.

Home, home, house to let! Deserted place
Keep away to stay alive,
Kissing wife by telephone call:
Leave my child in detention cell,
It's safer there than in our house,
Among the hippos spitting fire.

Home, new home! Where hopes are high.
Come back home South Africa is free,
On the ruins of John is Freedom Square:
Our dead are heroes; the living are free,
Black is color and white is paint,
To the glory of God and the good of man.

Home, permanent home! Where reunion dreams are realized.
Across the borders come our own,
From the island our very own:
Afflicted but not forgotten,
Imprisoned now free,
Next home mansions above.

Culture of evil, culture of loss

I told you in 1948
The year I lost my all
When I lost personhood

I had told you in 1910
The year we lost our unity
When they made their unity

I knew in 1838
As blood came down in flood
That it was only the beginning of the struggle.

I watched in 1833
As they trekked east and north
That next they would grab the whole land.

I was bent with age in 1652
When Van Riebeeck was a little man
That one day he would be a big problem.

My great-great-grandma was still queen,
Seven hundred years before they "discovered" the Cape
To call ours theirs.

It was in 1961 May 31
An illegitimate child was born
Named republic by Verwoerd now below the earth.

I predicted in 1960 March 21
When 69 offered their lives
Investment at the bank of freedom.

I wondered in 1976
As God paid supreme
How high the price before we fly.

I realized in 1984,
As I did in 1985,
That freedom would be a costly thing.

In 1986 I worked my balance sheet
Many boys and girls had paid
Men and women were up to date.

1987 found my hand on my chin
Stunned by facts in my computer machine
Children had overpaid their accounts.

I walked back a thousand and a thousand years
And saw him who paid my debt
Hanging there on the arms of a tree.

I watched tax collectors as they made us pay
As if the Golgotha cash was paid by check
By a cashier lost to sum in the fog.

A round around village and township
Young and old disappear
Losing limb and sense of belonging.

Over the fence and across the dusty street
Timely jump without a limb
Bitter gas against bitter anger.

Detention. Death. Madness. Loss.
Loss. Madness. Death. Detention.
Bitter anger against teargas.

I walked through the cemetery
Counting fresh graves marked by fisty stone
Of those lost and found.

I visited the mortuary and the cells
I tried hell and heaven
Even no-man's land in between.

I missed my son and longed for my daughter
I missed God and his two companions above
And tried the gods below.

I found no god above and no god below,
He was lost among his people,
Tearing the apartheid curtain between black and white.

Only one way to freedom

Naming us
Pushing us around
Painting us in borrowed colors
Fixing horns on our heads and tails between our legs
One head
One mouth
One nose
Two eyes
Two ears
Two legs that keep us way above the ground
In his image!

Starving us
Pushing us to the homelands
Forcing us to a status a little below the beast
Leaving rooms and roads and coasts to the Herrenvolk
One neck
One chest
One stomach
Two breasts
Two arms
Two buttocks stronger than the Immorality Act
In his likeness

Insulting us
Maiming us by fault and default intentionally
Reaping our fruits and raping our women
Culling us and killing elephants for crime of numbers
One people
One country
One hope
One struggle
One goal
One will to live stronger than the will to survive
In his footsteps

Denying us education we shall learn
Denying us information we shall know
Denying us vote we shall win
Crowded into 13% of the land we shall overflow
One nation

One loyalty
One government
Together beyond tribe
Together beyond race
Losing some battles in between, winning the final struggle
Back to the image of God
                In the land of peace
                Land of food and drink
                Lion and calf together
                Colors hand in hand.

Public enemy number one

If it were only an ugly word,
If we were dealing with a policy gone astray,
Or an ideology among others,
I would call professors together;
I would gather sociologists;
Anthropologists would explain the culture;
In a classroom or five star hotel;
Then we would learn and unlearn the past;
We would know what makes apartheid tick—
We would know the seed of greed—
We would know the secret of self-inflicted fear
That enslaves freedom fighters of old
Seated now on their neighbor's back.
    It is a religion: god in Satan's hand!

If it were only an election slogan,
If we were faced with ordinary human disease,
Or a temptation amongst ten,
I would appeal to Moses of old;
I would invite the wise from east and west;
From the north and south solutions would come;
As wise and fools mix fortunes in the same pot.
Then we would discover that reform will do—

That enriching the rich will not impoverish the poor—
That polishing the corpse of an apartheid shoe
Would give birth to a democratic boot.
Crushing the thorns that prick the soul,
Raising Lazarus from among the dead,
Giving hope to Martha and Mary.
   It is cancer.

If it were only Afrikaners behind the wheel,
If other whites would be like stainless steel,
Or at least neutral between wolf and flock,
I would appeal to conscience and science.
I would tap on English tradition.
French revolution would be no proper dose;
Talk to talk and not eye for an eye;
As we belabor from dawn to dusk,
All our needs and deeds of the past,
And find solutions before the gale.
Avoiding pains in the groin.
This patient is unlike others,
Like Hitler on the white horse,
Galloping down the precipice.
   It is suicide.
      Civil war.
         May be third world war.
           Hope not.
              Nats* are nuts.
                Watch!

---

*Nats: the ruling racist Nationalist party in South Africa since 1948.

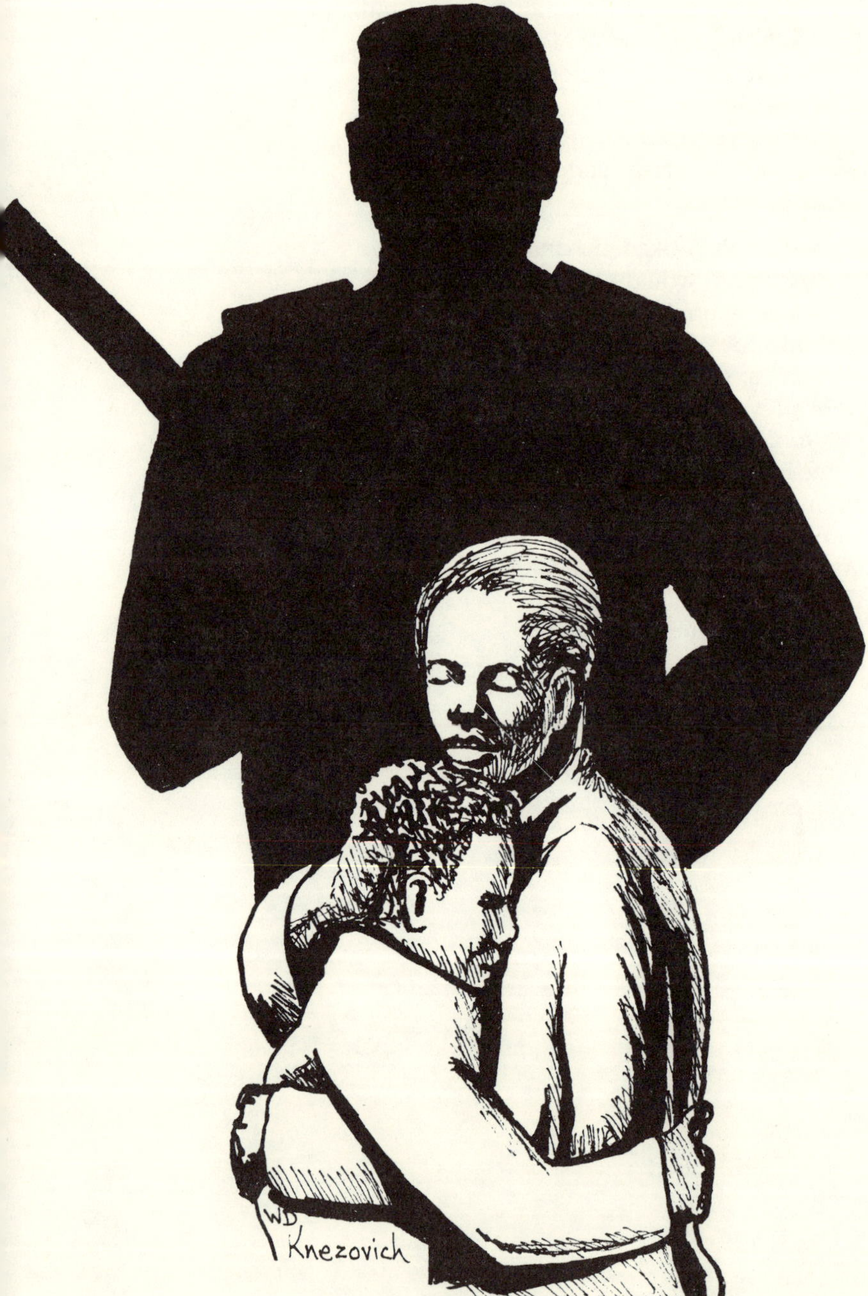
WD
Knezovich

Hostages: Mother Roxelelwa: We've lost

I do not know
Where my daughter is.
My son left yesterday and did not return.
If you know where my husband is let me know.

You will know
Where your daughter is.
Your son who left yesterday will have to return.
And it's not our business to know where your husband is.
   (Roxelelwa to herself):
   Nkululeko is under my bed
   Siyaya is underground
   Asikhathali, my husband, is held at Protea Police Station
   I do not know where my son and daughter are.

Today you know
You surely must know by now
Your daughter got it from you, like father like son
You know and you stay; you do not know you go
   (Roxelelwa to her 2 and 4 year old sons):
   Sechaba, you know nothing my little son.
   Mkonto, you are too young to understand.
   Grandma and grandpa are down six by four,
You: Criminals at two and four to Jo'burg prison.

Phalama kaffir bitch
Khwela terrorist puppies and all
Apples do not fall far from the tree
If they are yours you know where they are.
   Where to? Re ya kae mma?
   Under arrest my children. Re tswerwe banaka.
   What does arrest mean mummy? Go tswarwa ke eng mma?
   Only police know my children. Go tseba sekuriti banaka.

Dear God: A telephone call to heaven

Heaven number one?
Yes!
Who's speaking?
Gabriel!
May I speak to God?
He is not here!
Jesus?
Not here!
The Holy Spirit?
Not here!
When will they be home?
They have no home!
May I leave a message with you?
No!
Why not?
It is not my duty!
Am I speaking with heaven?
Yes!
Why can't I reach God?
He does not live here!
Where can I find him?
Everywhere!
He is not here.
Where are you?
In South Africa.
He is also there!
We've been looking for him since 1652.
He is there!
No. He is not here. Tell Him on his return that
Mandela is in prison for life, and many more;
Sixty-nine were shot by Christian forces on March 21, 1960;
Six hundred students died in 1976;
Steve Biko died in detention in 1977;
Many more before and after that;
Tens of thousands have been detained between 1984 and 1987;
Children and adults;
Thousands have died;
The black version of his image has become baboon;
The disease of Ham has turned into an epidemic among blacks;

We are hewing wood;
We are drawing water;
Cursed to the hundredth and millionth generation;
White man's Bible declares:
Pharaoh is on the rampage;
We are scattered in his fields;
We build pyramids;
We put up cities;
Forced to say thanks for every kick;
We sacrifice our sons to the sun god;
Only Moses is left among the reeds.
On His way to the moon, let Him stop here for a day,
To see for Himself what we've seen for years.

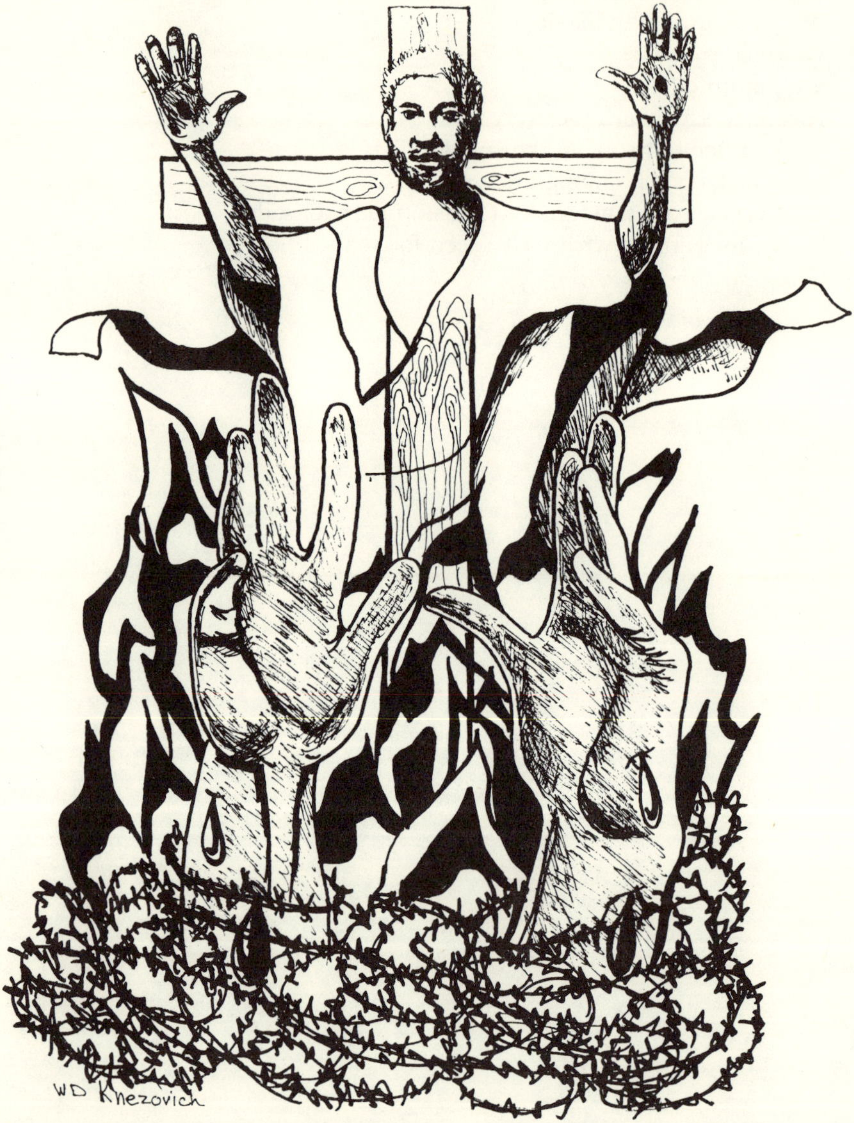
WD Knezovich

Victory is certain

Unzima lomthwalo:
The burden is heavy.
U funa amadoda:
It calls for men.
U funa sibambane:
It calls for unity.
Asikhathali:
We do not mind.
Noma siyabotshwa:
Going to jail.
Sisimisele:
We are committed to.
Inkululekho:
Our freedom.

Interrogation is born of weakness.
Intimidation descendant of insecurity.
Harassment is born of confusion,
Detention of unbridled fear.
Wrong on top you are below;
Below and right you are on top.
Is the struggle continuing?
Victory is coming.
Is victory coming?
The struggle must continue.

A   F   V
l   o   i
u   r   c
t   w   t
a   a   o
      r   r
c   d   y
o
n   w   i
t   i   s
i   t
n   h   c
u   e
a   t   r
      h   t
      e   a
            i
      s   n
      t
      r
      u
      g
      g
      l
      e

Enough for everybody

Gold is not scarce;
It is controlled.
Diamonds are not precious;
They are polished.

Little boys we fought for little girls,
Little girls we quarrelled for little boys.
    Why?
There is enough for everybody.

Little Nzumbu fought little Ndamu,
Little Ndamu fought little Zwo.
    Why?
There is enough candy for every kid.

Little hummingbird stung by bumblebee,
Little red finch attacked by big grosbeal.
    Why?
There is enough nectar and grain for everybody.

Big nation trampling small nation,
Super power against non-power.
    Why?
There is enough room for everybody.

Go home, whitey, go home,
Back to the ghetto blackie, to your place little nigger.
    Why?
There is enough humanity for everybody.
    ENOUGH
    ENOUGH
God's love for everybody.

Does it matter

Does it matter
That you were secretary of the Venda Students' Association?
You are not a hero.

Does it matter
That you were a paper decorator in SASO?[1]
You are not a hero.

Does it matter
That you were BPC[2] president?
You are not a hero.

Does it matter
That you were BECO[3] president?
You are not a hero.

Does it matter
That you are dean?
You are not a hero.

Does it matter
That you were inmate two score minus thirty-six?
You are not a hero.

Does it matter
That you were never excommunicated?
You are not an angel.

Coward and brave walk hand in hand in me;
Fear and courage are neighbors in me.
I am man of flesh and blood.
    GOD IS SPIRIT.

---

[1] SASO: South African Students Association.
[2] BPC: Black People's Convention.
[3] BECO: Bold Evangelical Christian Organization.

Above the law

Pope—Archbishop
  Dean
    Pastor
      Evangelist
        Deaconess
          Layperson
            Everybody
Not immune to state power.
Everybody
  President—Prime Minister
    Chairperson
      Executive officer
        Rank and file
Not immune to security power.
Dead
  Emperor—King—Queen
    Living
      Dying
        Being born
Not immune to the law.
Only
  Special branch
    Security police
Are above the law.

The mind of a detainee

He is not just one of them
   One among the unfortunate.
He is not a statistic number fifty thousand
   One among apartheid victims.
He is not one among the countless casualties
   one of the disappeared.
         He has a soul.
         He has a body.
            He
            has
            a
         MIND
         MIND?

He sits alone feeling lonely
   One among feelers.
He counts himself priority number one
   One Zwelakhe son of Sisulu.
   One unlike no other.
         He has a soul.
         He has a body.
            He
            has
            a
         MIND
         MIND?

He trembles in a cold cell
   Would love a shawl left at home.
He vomits for his bowels rebel
   They know of better days.
He sees a face and hugs the air
   To one in two is one cursed is the cold night unshared.
         He has a soul.
         He has a body.
            He
            has
            a
         MIND
         MIND?

He would like to go if wishes were horses
   To ride on last night's dream.
He would like to fly like the crow that sings and goes
   Except that he is not an angel yet.
If that key's path and his would cross
   No one would cross freedom's path before his chest.

He

has

a

MIND

that minds his soul

a

SOUL

that enlivens his body

a

BODY

that carries his soul

a

SOUL

a

BODY

and

MIND

that they call DETAINEE.

From the mouth of those that sow in our midst

        How
Many pagans do you have in your country?
        Where
did you buy the beautiful skirt that you wear?
        How
do you do it: we hear people jump from tree to tree in Africa?
        We
Use... we use... we use... we use... EVELATORS.
        What
do you eat in your country?
        Do
your kids like our food?
        Why
do you people come here and buy expensive clothes when
        We
know your people are suffering and starving?
        We
need your brains and charity to keep us afloat.
        What
are your academic credentials
        that
entitle you to say what you tell us?
        Where
did Bishop Tutu and Boesak
        learn
all that they preach to the gullible world?
        WITHOUT
your universities we can only dream
        WITHOUT
the right skin our CREDENTIALS are irrevocably suspect.
        How
        LARGE
are you families in AFRICA, is
        FOURTEEN
children per family the normal size?
        You
        SEEM
somewhat clear in your thinking logic
        Are
        YOU

an exception—a—deviant among your own?
            NOT
made in His IMAGE surely I must be an exception
            Why
            are
            Black
            governments
so ill-advised and narrow-minded?
            BEFORE
Uhuru we ate WELL and had all we needed:
            FOURTEEN
courses per DINNER in those golden days:
            WHEN
We were good FRIENDS with South Africa
            IMPORTING
goods and gadgets almost for nothing:
            ENTERTAINING
DUTCH REFORMED CLERGY THAT FREQUENTED OUR SHORES
            Why
            Why
   That IS all gone?
            BUT
   You ARE still there.
            Now
            May
            I
            ask
Why-why-why-why-only why?
            He
Went to the service the other day
            From
Thousands miles across the horizons
            sat
in front as prominent as his nose was flat
            but
was as invisible as the sun on a cloudless day?
            Now
            He
            is
at home away from home
in the BAPTIST church
            How
            not

        Only
        Why
that five souls OF the same creed
       afflicted
       SOULS
  from across the shores
       SHARED
the blood and the bread of life
from your Hand in your church
twenty Sundays in as many weeks
       WITHOUT
A word of love, of comfort or of welcome
      If
Luther were God I would search for another.
       Come
       to
       the
       Lake
this very evening to talk of your woes
      to
      strangers
      that
  come and go
      My
Congregation too holy for that.
      Now
      Know
this, my fellow Lutheran cleric:
      I
  am no teller of tales:
      Teller
of the Gospel as you are so am I.
      If
my Gospel is not good for your flock
      then
your flock is not good for me.
      When
you came we let you preach.
      After
you preached we let you talk.
      Not
that we liked everything you said
      not

that we found no fault with your theology
         but
who are we to deny the flock the right to hear.
         Without
hearing there is no right to decide.

On my heels

They
chase my thoughts
They
ban my ideas
My
letters they read
everyday

When
I preach an informer records
When
I speak recorders squeak
My
prayers guilty of incitement
Blasphemous

JFK
Not safe in New York
In
the capitol Washington
Tape recorder
that the listener's briefcase ready for me
Persecuted

Only
Presidents have escorts
Premiers
Only have bodyguards
Why
me little shadow that I am
overrated!

Bloodstains in my hand

Not from my nose,
Not from my wound,
   bloodstains in my hand?

Not from an enemy,
Not from a foe,
   Bloodstains in my hand?

I shook a friend's hand,
I embraced a colleague
   And got bloodstains in my hand.

Can a laugh cause this big wound?
A hug this disjointed shoulder?
   Friendly gesture a spear through my heart?

They kill not easily that threaten to kill,
They kill easy that pretend to love,
   He felled two with a laugh last night.

He pulled me to him in the name of brotherhood;
She bundled me in a twiggy smile,
   For fire in the icy season.

Oh my palm! Bloodstained palm!
Oh my enemy, lovecoated poison!
   If only you had frowned on me!

Is it too late to hate you?
Is it too late to love those I hated?
   I hate to make a decision,
   But for how long can I suspend myself?

Home-sick

I
became man on mother's milk:
Milk
that makes me sick when sister little sucks
On
Mother's breast that once was
Mine:
I
long for my home where:
I lay
my head between the two
that
now
feed another before my eyes.
I . . . I?
became a stranger among my own:
Body
of Christ that make me feel like a
Branch
detached from the stem.
I . . . I?
feel like a stem rejected by the
Roots
of those who sprouted the word on
our shores
to
show the way they've never
Trodden,
I . . . I?
know for sure before they came
One
thing we know was love without bias.